TRAVELING LIGHT

Traveling Light
Collected and New Poems

David Wagoner

University of Illinois Press
Urbana and Chicago

Manufactured in the United States of America

1 2 3 4 5 C P 5 4 3 2

♾ This book is printed on acid-free paper.

Library of Congress Cataloging-in-Publication Data
Wagoner, David.
Traveling light : collected and new poems / David Wagoner.
p. cm.
ISBN 0-252-02488-5 (acid-free paper)
ISBN 0-252-06803-3 (paperback : acid-free paper)
I. Title.
PS3545.A345T69   1999
811'.54—dc21   98-58032
CIP

These poems are all for
Robin, Alexandra, and Addy,
with all my love

Contents

Two

From *Who Shall Be the Sun?* (1978)

From *Through the Forest: New and Selected Poems, 1977–87*

One

Two

Three

Four

Five

From *Walt Whitman Bathing* (1996)

One

From *Collected Poems, 1956–76*

The Words

Wind, bird, and tree,
Water, grass, and light:
In half of what I write
Roughly or smoothly
Year by impatient year,
The same six words recur.

I have as many floors
As meadows or rivers,
As much still air as wind
And as many cats in mind
As nests in the branches
To put an end to these.

Instead, I take what is:
The light beats on the stones,
And wind over water shines
Like long grass through the trees,
As I set loose, like birds
In a landscape, the old words.

Staying Alive

Staying alive in the woods is a matter of calming down
At first and deciding whether to wait for rescue,
Trusting to others,
Or simply to start walking and walking in one direction
Till you come out—or something happens to stop you.
By far the safer choice
Is to settle down where you are, and try to make a living
Off the land, camping near water, away from shadows.
Eat no white berries;
Spit out all bitterness. Shooting at anything
Means hiking further and further every day
To hunt survivors;
It may be best to learn what you have to learn without a gun,
Not killing but watching birds and animals go
In and out of shelter
At will. Following their example, build for a whole season:
Facing across the wind in your lean-to,
You may feel wilder,
But nothing, not even you, will have to stay in hiding.
If you have no matches, a stick and a fire-bow
Will keep you warmer,
Or the crystal of your watch, filled with water, held up to the sun
Will do the same in time. In case of snow
Drifting toward winter,
Don't try to stay awake through the night, afraid of freezing—
The bottom of your mind knows all about zero;
It will turn you over
And shake you till you waken. If you have trouble sleeping
Even in the best of weather, jumping to follow
With eyes strained to their corners
The unidentifiable noises of the night and feeling
Bears and packs of wolves nuzzling your elbow,
Remember the trappers
Who treated them indifferently and were left alone.
If you hurt yourself, no one will comfort you
Or take your temperature,

So stumbling, wading, and climbing are as dangerous as flying.
But if you decide, at last, you must break through
In spite of all danger,
Think of yourself by time and not by distance, counting
Wherever you're going by how long it takes you;
No other measure
Will bring you safe to nightfall. Follow no streams: they run
Under the ground or fall into wilder country.
Remember the stars
And moss when your mind runs into circles. If it should rain
Or the fog should roll the horizon in around you,
Hold still for hours
Or days if you must, or weeks, for seeing is believing
In the wilderness. And if you find a pathway,
Wheel rut, or fence wire,
Retrace it left or right: someone knew where he was going
Once upon a time, and you can follow
Hopefully, somewhere,
Just in case. There may even come, on some uncanny evening,
A time when you're warm and dry, well fed, not thirsty,
Uninjured, without fear,
When nothing, either good or bad, is happening.
This is called staying alive. It's temporary.
What occurs after
Is doubtful. You must always be ready for something to come bursting
Through the far edge of a clearing, running toward you,
Grinning from ear to ear
And hoarse with welcome. Or something crossing and hovering
Overhead, as light as air, like a break in the sky,
Wondering what you are.
Here you are face to face with the problem of recognition.
Having no time to make smoke, too much to say,
You should have a mirror
With a tiny hole in the back for better aiming, for reflecting
Whatever disaster you can think of, to show
The way you suffer.
These body signals have universal meaning: If you are lying
Flat on your back with arms outstretched behind you,
You say you require
Emergency treatment; if you are standing erect and holding
Arms horizontal, you mean you are not ready;

If you hold them over
Your head, you want to be picked up. Three of anything
Is a sign of distress. Afterward, if you see
No ropes, no ladders,
No maps or messages falling, no searchlights or trails blazing,
Then, chances are, you should be prepared to burrow
Deep for a deep winter.

Talking to the Forest

When we can understand animals, we will know the change is halfway.
When we can talk to the forest, we will know that the change has come.
—*Andrew Joe, Skagit Tribe, Washington*

We'll notice first they've quit turning their ears
To catch our voices drifting through cage bars,
The whites of their eyes no longer shining from corners.
And all dumb animals suddenly struck dumb
Will turn away, embarrassed by a change
Among our hoots and catcalls, whistles and snorts
That crowd the air as tightly as ground-mist.

The cassowary pacing the hurricane fence,
The owl on the driftwood, the gorilla with folding arms,
The buffalo aimed all day in one direction,
The bear on his rock—will need no talking to,
Spending their time so deeply wrapped in time
(Where words lie down like the lion and the lamb)
Not even their own language could reach them.

And so, we'll have to get out of the zoo
To the forest, rain or shine, whichever comes
Dropping its downright shafts before our eyes,
And think of something to say, using new words
That won't turn back bewildered, lost or scattered
Or panicked, curling under the first bush
To wait for a loud voice to hunt them out,

Not words that fall from the skin looking like water
And running together, meaning anything,
Then disappearing into the forest floor
Through gray-green moss and ferns rotting in shade,
Not words like crown-fire overhead, but words
Like old trees felled by themselves in the wilderness,
Making no noise unless someone is listening.

Talking to Barr Creek

Under the peach-leaf willows, alders, and choke cherries,
By coltsfoot, devil's club, sweet-after-death,
And bittersweet nightshade,
Like a fool, I sit here talking to you, begging a favor,
A lesson as hard and long as your bed of stones
To hold me together.
At first, thinking of you, my mind slid down like a leaf
From source to mouth, as if you were only one
Piece of yourself at a time,
As if you were nowhere but here or there, nothing but now,
One place, one measure. But you are all at once,
Beginning through ending.
What man could look at you all day and not be a beggar?
How could he take his eyes at their face value?
How could his body
Bear its dead weight? Grant me your endless, ungrudging impulse
Forward, the lavishness of your light movements,
Your constant inconstancy,
Your leaping and shallowing, your stretches of black and amber,
Bluing and whitening, your long-drawn wearing away,
Your sudden stillness.
From the mountain lake ten miles uphill to the broad river,
Teach me your spirit, going yet staying, being
Born, vanishing, enduring.

Do Not Proceed Beyond This Point without a Guide

The official warning, nailed to a hemlock,
Doesn't say why. I stand with my back to it,
Afraid I've come as far as I can
By being stubborn, and look
Downward for miles at the hazy crags and spurs.

A rubble-covered ridge like a bombed stairway
Leads up beyond the sign. It doesn't
Seem any worse than what I've climbed already.
Why should I have to take a guide along
To watch me scaring myself to death?

What was it I wanted? A chance to look around
On a high rock already named and numbered
By somebody else? A chance to shout
Over the heads of people who quit sooner?
Shout what? I can't go tell it on the mountain.

I sit for a while, raking the dead leaves
Out of my lungs and traveling lightheaded
Downward again in my mind's eye, till there's nothing
Left of my feet but rags and bones
And nothing to look down on but my shoes.

The closer I come to it, the harder it is to doubt
How well this mountain can take me or leave me.
The hemlock had more sense. It stayed where it was,
Grew up and down at the same time, branch and root,
Being a guide instead of needing one.

Lost

Stand still. The trees ahead and bushes beside you
Are not lost. Wherever you are is called Here,
And you must treat it as a powerful stranger,
Must ask permission to know it and be known.
The forest breathes. Listen. It answers,
I have made this place around you.
If you leave it, you may come back again, saying Here.
No two trees are the same to Raven.
No two branches are the same to Wren.
If what a tree or a bush does is lost on you,
You are surely lost. Stand still. The forest knows
Where you are. You must let it find you.

Sleeping in the Woods

Not having found your way out of the woods, begin
Looking for somewhere to bed down at nightfall
Though you have nothing
But part of yourself to lie on, nothing but skin and backbone
And the bare ungiving ground to reconcile.
From standing to kneeling,
From crouching to turning over old leaves, to going under,
You must help yourself like any animal
To enter the charmed circle
Of the night with a body not meant for stretching or sprawling:
One ear flap at a time knuckling your skull,
Your stiff neck (needing
An owl's twist to stay even) cross-purposing your spine,
With rigid ankles, with nowhere to put your arms.
But now, lying still
At last, you may watch the shadows seeking their own level,
The ground beneath you neither rising nor falling,
Neither giving nor taking
From the dissolving cadence of your heart, identical darkness
Behind and before your eyes—and you are going
To sleep without a ceiling,
For the first time without walls, not *falling* asleep, not losing
Anything under you to the imponderable
Dead and living
Earth, your countervailing bed, but settling down
Beside it across the slackening threshold
Of the place where it is always
Light, at the beginning of dreams, where the stars, shut out
By leaves and branches in another forest, burn
At the mattering source
Forever, though a dream may have its snout half sunk in blood
And the mind's tooth gnaw all night at bone and tendon
Among the trembling snares:
Whoever stumbles across you in the dark may borrow
Your hidebound substance for the encouragement
Of mites or angels;

But whatever they can't keep is yours for the asking. Turn up
In time, at the first faint stretch of dawn, and you'll see
A world pale-green as hazel,
The chalk-green convolute lichen by your hand like sea fog,
The fallen tree beside you in half-light
Dreaming a greener sapling,
The dead twigs turning over, and your cupped hand lying open
Beyond you in the morning like a flower.
Making light of it,
You have forgotten why you came, have served your purpose, and simply
By being here have found the right way out.
Now, you may waken.

Working against Time

By the newly bulldozed logging road, for a hundred yards,
I saw the sprawling five-foot hemlocks, their branches crammed
Into each other's light, upended or wrenched aslant
Or broken across waists the size of broomsticks
Or bent, crushed slewfoot on themselves in the duff like briars,
Their roots coming at random out of the dirt, and dying.

I had no burlap in the trunk, not even a spade,
And the shirt off my back wasn't enough to go around.
I'm no tree surgeon, it wasn't Arbor Day, but I climbed
Over the free-for-all, untangling winners and losers
And squeezing as many as I could into my car.
When I started, nothing was singing in the woods except me.

I hardly had room to steer—roots dangled over my shoulder
And scraped the side of my throat as if looking for water.
Branches against the fog on the windshield dabbled designs
Like kids or hung out the vent. The sun was falling down.
It's against the law to dig up trees. Working against
Time and across laws, I drove my ambulance

Forty miles in the dark to the house and began digging
Knee-deep graves for most of them, while the splayed headlights
Along the highway picked me out of the night:
A fool with a shovel searching for worms or treasure,
Both buried behind the sweat on his forehead. Two green survivors
Are tangled under the biting rain as I say this.

One Ear to the Ground

Stretched out on the ground, I hear the news of the night
Pass over and under:
The faraway honks of geese flying blind as stars
(And hoof- or heartbeats),
The squeaks of bats, impaling moths in the air,
Who leave light wings
To flutter by themselves down to the grass
(And under that grass
The thud and thump of meeting, the weasel's whisper),
Through the crackling thorns
Over creekbeds up the ridge and against the moon,
The coyotes howling
All national anthems, cresting, picking up
Where men leave off
(And, beneath, the rumble of faulted and flawed earth
Shaking its answer).

Report from a Forest Logged by the Weyerhaeuser Company

Three square miles clear-cut.
Now only the facts matter:
The heaps of gray-splintered rubble,
The churned-up duff, the roots, the bulldozed slash,
The silence,

And beyond the ninth hummock
(All of them pitched sideways like wrecked houses)
A creek still running somewhere, bridged and dammed
By cracked branches.
No birdsong. Not one note.

And this is April, a sunlit morning.
Nothing but facts. Wedges like half-moons
Fallen where saws cut over and under them
Bear ninety or more rings.
A trillium gapes at so much light.

Among the living: a bent huckleberry,
A patch of salal, a wasp,
And now, making a mistake about me,
Two brown-and-black butterflies landing
For a moment on my boot.

Among the dead: thousands of fir seedlings
A foot high, planted ten feet apart,
Parched brown for lack of the usual free rain,
Two buckshot beer cans, and overhead,
A vulture big as an eagle.

Selective logging, they say, we'll take three miles,
It's good for the bears and deer, they say,
More brush and berries sooner or later,
We're thinking about the future—if you're in it
With us, they say. It's a comfort to say

Like *Dividend* or *Forest Management* or *Keep Out*.
They've managed this to a fare-thee-well.

Riverbed

1

Through the salt mouth of the river
They come past the dangling mesh of gillnets
And the purse-mouthed seines, past the fishermen's last strands
By quarter-light where the beheaded herring
Spiral against the tide, seeing the shadowy others
Hold still, then slash, then rise to the surface, racked
And disappearing—now deepening slowly
In the flat mercurial calm of the pulp mills, groping
Half clear at last and rising like the stones below them
Through swifter and swifter water, the salmon returning
By night or morning in the white rush from the mountains,
Hunting, in the thresh and welter of creek mouths
And shifting channels, the one true holding place.

Out of our smoke and clangor, these miles uphill,
We come back to find them, to wait at their nesting hollows
With the same unreasoning hope.

2

We walk on round stones, all flawlessly bedded,
Where water drags the cracked dome of the sky
Downstream a foot at a glance, to falter there
Like caught leaves, quivering over the sprint
Of the current, the dashing of surfaces.

In a month of rain, the water will rise above
Where we stand on a curving shelf below an island—
The blue daylight scattered and the leaves
All castaways like us for a season.
The river turns its stones like a nesting bird
From hollow to hollow. Now gulls and ravens
Turn to the salmon stranded among branches.

They lie in the clear shallows, the barely dead,
While some still beat their flanks white for the spawning,
And we lie down all day beside them.

Fire by the River

We gather wood, the bleached, clay-covered branches
As heavy as fossils, drag them to the shore,
    And cross them, touching a match
To a nest of twigs. And the fire begins between us
Under this evening kindled by our breath.

It gathers dusk in tight against our backs,
Lighting us half by half. The river roars
    Like a fire drawn through a valley.
The smoke pours down to the water's edge like a creek
And empties into the broad, downstreaming night.

The first chill draws our arms around each other.
Like firelight under eyelids, the stars spread out.
    We lie down with ourselves.
The lighted halves of our bodies sink together.
The moon leans inward, banking on darkness.

Set free by our sleep and coming down to the water,
The bears, the deer, the martens dark as their fur,
    As soundless as night herons,
All drink and turn away, making no light.
The tail of the wind is stirring the soft ashes,

And nothing of ours will be left in the morning
Though we guard it now through dewfall and ground-mist.
    But here at the heart of night
A salmon leaps: the smack of his wild body
Breaks through the valley, splashing our sleep with fire.

The Lesson

That promising morning
Driving beside the river,
I saw twin newborn lambs
Still in a daze
At the grassy sunlight;
Beyond them, a day-old colt
As light-hoofed as the mare
That swayed over his muzzle—
Three staggering new lives
Above the fingerlings
From a thousand salmon nests—
And I sang on the logging road
Uphill for miles, then came
To a fresh two thousand acres
Of a familiar forest
Clear-cut and left for dead
By sawtoothed Weyerhaeuser.

I haunted those gray ruins
For hours, listening to nothing,
Being haunted in return
By vacancy, vacancy,
Till I grew as gray as stumps
Cut down to size. They drove me
Uphill, steeper and steeper,
Thinking: the salmon will die
In gillnets and crude oil,
The colt be broken and broken,
And the lambs leap to their slaughter.

I found myself in a rage
Two-thirds up Haystack Mountain
Being buzzed and ricochetted
By a metallic whir
That jerked me back toward life
Among young firs and cedars—
By a rufous hummingbird
Exulting in wild dives
For a mate perched out of sight
And cackling over and over,
Making me crouch and cringe
In his fiery honor.

Standing Halfway Home

At the last turn in the path, where locust thorns
Halter my sleeve, I suddenly stand still
For no good reason, planting both my shoes.
No other takes its place when my noise ends.
The hush is on. Through the deserted boughs,
Through fireweed, bracken, duff, down to the ground,
The air comes as itself without a sound
And deepens at my knees like waste of breath.

Behind my back lies the end of property;
Ahead, around a corner, a new house.
Barbed wire and aerials cross up and out
To mark the thresholds of man's common sense:
Keep out, keep talking. Doing neither one,
Here, central and inert, I stop my mouth
To reassure all the invisible
For whom my sight and sound were dangerous.

Eyes in the wings of butterflies stare through
The hazel leaves. Frozen beside my foot,
A tawny skink relaxes on its toes.
I shift my weight. The sun bears down the hill,
And overhead, past where an eye can turn,
A hiss of feathers parts the silence now.
At my arm's length a seedy, burr-sized wren,
As if I were a stalk, bursts into song.

The Gathering of the Loons

In the dead calm before darkness near the shore
The loons are gathering, rippling blue-gray
As slow as driftwood, the lighthouse blinking
And sweeping across the long calls of the gulls,
The scoters darkening, the breathlessly sighing
Wingbeats of goldeneyes across the marsh grass
Lifting the widgeons up in gold-streaked wedges
To take one way toward night against the mountains,
And the still loons, the solitary loons
Drifting together out into the bay,
The silent loons all floating toward sleep.

An Offering for Dungeness Bay

1

The tern, his lean, slant wings
Swiveling, lifts and hovers
Over the glassy bay,
Then plunges suddenly into that breaking mirror,
Into himself, and rises, bearing silver
In his beak and trailing silver
Falling to meet itself over and over.

2

Over the slow surf
Where the moon is opening,
Begin, the plover cries,
And beyond the shallows
The far-off answer,
Again, again, again,
Under the white wind
And the long boom of the breakers
Where the still whiter branches
Lie pitched and planted deep,
Only begin, the water says,
And the rest will follow.

3

Dusk and low tide and the sanderlings
Alighting in their hundreds by the last of the light
On sea wrack floating in the final ripples
Lightly, scarcely touching, and now telling
This night, *Here,* and this night coming,
Here, where we are, as their beaks turn down and thin,
As fine as sand grains, *Here is the place.*

4

The geese at the brim of darkness are beginning
To rise from the bay, a few at first in formless
Clusters low to the water, their black wings beating
And whistling like shorebirds to bear them up, and calling
To others, to others as they circle wider
Over the shelving cove, and now they gather
High toward the marsh in chevrons and echelons,
Merging and interweaving, their long necks turning
Seaward and upward, catching a wash of moonlight
And rising farther and farther, stretching away,
Lifting, beginning again, going on and on.

A Guide to Dungeness Spit

Out of wild roses down from the switching road between pools
We step to an arm of land washed from the sea.
On the windward shore
The combers come from the strait, from narrows and shoals
Far below sight. To leeward, floating on trees
In a blue cove, the cormorants
Stretch to a point above us, their wings held out like sky-sails.
Where shall we walk? First, put your prints to the sea,
Fill them, and pause there:
Seven miles to the lighthouse, curved yellow-and-gray miles
Tossed among kelp, abandoned with bleaching roof-trees,
Past reaches and currents;
And we must go afoot at a time when the tide is heeling.
Those whistling overhead are Canada geese;
Some on the waves are loons,
And more on the sand are pipers. There, Bonaparte's gulls
Settle a single perch. Those are sponges.
Those are the ends of bones.
If we cross to the inner shore, the grebes and goldeneyes
Rear themselves and plunge through the still surface,
Fishing below the dunes
And rising alarmed, higher than waves. Those are cockleshells.
And these are the dead. I said we would come to these.
Stoop to the stones.
Overturn one: the gray-and-white, inch-long crabs come pulsing
And clambering from their hollows, tiptoeing sideways.
They lift their pincers
To defend the dark. Let us step this way. Follow me closely
Past snowy plovers bustling among sand fleas.
The air grows dense.
You must decide now whether we shall walk for miles and miles
And whether all birds are the young of other creatures
Or their own young ones,
Or simply their old selves because they die. One falls,
And the others touch him webfoot or with claws,
Treading him for the ocean.

This is called sanctuary. Those are feathers and scales.
We both go into mist, and it hooks behind us.
Those are foghorns.
Wait, and the bird on the high root is a snowy owl
Facing the sea. Its flashing yellow eyes
Turn past us and return;
And turning from the calm shore to the breakers, utterly still,
They lead us by the bay and through the shallows,
Buoy us into the wind.
Those are tears. Those are called houses, and those are people.
Here is a stairway past the whites of our eyes.
All our distance
Has ended in the light. We climb to the light in spirals,
And look, between us we have come all the way,
And it never ends
In the ocean, the spit and image of our guided travels.
Those are called ships. We are called lovers.
There lie the mountains.

The Osprey's Nest

The osprey's nest has dropped of its own weight
After years, breaking everything under it, collapsing
Out of the sky like the wreckage of the moon,
Having killed its branch and rotted its lodgepole:
A flying cloud of fishbones tall as a man,
A shambles of dead storms ten feet across.

Uncertain what holds anything together,
Ospreys try everything—fishnets and broomsticks,
Welcome mats and pieces of scarecrows,
Sheep bones, shells, the folded wings of mallards—
And heap up generations till they topple.

In the nest the young ones, calling fish to fly
Over the water toward them in old talons,
Thought only of hunger diving down their throats
To the heart, not letting go—(not letting go,
Ospreys have washed ashore, ruffled and calm
But drowned, their claws embedded in salmon).
They saw the world was bones and curtain rods,
Hay-wire and cornstalks—rubble put to bed
And glued into meaning by large appetites.
Living on top of everything that mattered,
The fledglings held it in the air with their eyes,
With awkward claws groping the ghosts of fish.

Last night they slapped themselves into the wind
And cried across the rain, flopping for comfort
Against the nearest branches, baffled by leaves
And the blank darkness falling below their breasts.
Where have they gone? The nest, now heaped on the bank,
Has come to earth smelling as high as heaven.

Observations from the Outer Edge

I pass the abrupt end of the woods, and stop.
I'm standing on a cliff as sheer as a step
Where the ground, like the ground floor of a nightmare,
Has slipped a notch six hundred rocky feet
And left itself in the lurch. My shoes go dead.
Not looking yet, I let my heart sneak back,

But feel like the fall guy ending a Western,
The heavy, bound to topple from the edge
And disappear with terrible gravity.
I put my hand out in the separate air
With nothing under it, but it feels nothing.
This is no place for putting my foot down,

So I shout my name, but can't scare up an echo.
No one inside this canyon wants to be me.
I manage to look down. Not much to envy:
The silent, immobile rapids, the toy pines,
A fisherman stuck in the shallows like an agate—
A world so far away, it could quit moving

And I wouldn't know the difference. I've seen it before
At the ends of hallways, the far sides of windows,
Shrinking from sight. Down is no worse than across.
Whether it's sky, horizon, or ground zero,
A piece of space will take whatever comes
From any direction—climbing, walking, or falling.

I remember a newsreel—a man holding a baby
Over the Grand Canyon on a stick:
The kid hung on and grinned for the camera.
I grab the nearest branch just to make sure
It isn't death down there, looking like hell.
Even a mountain goat will go to pieces

Standing on glass suspended in the air,
But man created with a jerkier balance
Can learn to fix his eyes on a safe place.
Trembling somewhere,
The acrophobiac Primum Mobile
Clings to his starry axle, staring sideways.

The Other Side of the Mountain

To walk downhill you must lean partially backward,
Heels digging in,
While your body gets more help than it can use
In following directions—
Because it's possible simply to fall down
The way you're going
Instead of climbing against it. The baffling dead ends
Of traveling upward
Are turned around now, their openings leading down
To the land you promised
Yourself, beyond box canyons and blind draws.
They branch repeatedly,
But the direction you choose should be as easy to take
As your right hand.
The sky is a constant; even its variables
Like cirrus and cumulus
Will cancel each other out in a rough balance,
Taking turns at weather.
The wind may bluff and bluster and cut corners
Or skip a whole valley,
But eventually it has nothing to do with you,
Not even when it throws
The dust of your own country in your eyes.
At dawn, at darkness,
The sun will be here or there, full-face, rear-view;
It evens out in the end.
You must keep your goal in mind as clear as day
Though it doesn't matter
What you may think it looks like: second sight
Is simply perseverance;
And getting there from here is a set of stages
Demanding candlepower,
Foot-pounds and simple levers, thirst and hunger.
Signposts are seasonal
And not forensic: one end may come to a point
And the other be indented,

But the words will be gone, and the rusty earth and air
Will have eaten the pole and nails.
You must take time to notice what grows on rocks
Or squeezes between them—
The gnawing lichen, bone-weed and thorny scrub—
All hanging tough
And gnarling for elbowroom or squatters' rights.
These are the straighteners,
The levelers at work on the thick and crooked:
Some distant species
Will find the world made flat by the likes of these.
You must do your bit
By scuffing downhill heel-first on behalf of erosion,
For the sake of another time
When the mountains are made plain and anyone standing
Can see from here to there
Without half trying. When your shoes are out of step
And your clothes are a burden
And you feel bone-tired, sit down and look around.
You're there. No matter what
You had in mind as a proper circumstance,
You've come to it at last:
A rock-strewn slope from which you have a view
Of a further rock-strewn slope.
You can pick up dust in your hand and let it fall.
The place is real.
You can bite a grass stem, look, take a deep breath
And, naturally, let it go.

Tumbleweed

Here comes another, bumping over the sage
Among the greasewood, wobbling diagonally
Downhill, then skimming a moment on edge,
Tilting lopsided, bouncing end over end
And springing from the puffs of its own dust
To catch at the barbed wire
And hang there, shaking, like a riddled prisoner.

Half the sharp seeds have fallen from this tumbler,
Knocked out for good by headstands and pratfalls
Between here and wherever it grew up.
I carry it in the wind across the road
To the other fence. It jerks in my hands,
Butts backward, corkscrews, lunges and swivels,
Then yaws away as soon as it's let go,
Hopping the scrub uphill like a kicked maverick.
The air goes hard and straight through the wires and weeds.
Here comes another, flopping among the sage.

Water Music for the Progress of Love in a Life Raft Down the Sammamish Slough

Slipping at long last from the shore, we wave
    To no one in a house
With a dismantled chimney, a sprung gate,
    And five bare windows,
And begin this excursion under thorny vines
    Trailing like streamers
Over the mainstream, in our inflated life raft,
    Bluer and yellower
Than the sky and sun which hold the day together.
    My love, upstream,
Be the eyes behind me, saying yes and no.
    I'm manning the short oars
Which must carry us with the current, or without it,
    Six miles to our pasture.
There go the mallards patched with gray and white
    By their tame fathers;
Down from the leaves the kingfishers branching go
    Raucous under the willows
And out of sight; the star-backed salmon are waiting
    For the rain to rise above us;
And the wind is sending our raft like a water spider
    Skimming over the surface.
We begin our lesson here, our slight slow progress,
    Sitting face to face,
Able to touch our hands or soaking feet
    But not to kiss
As long as we must wait at opposite ends,
    Keeping our balance,
Our spirits cold as the Sammamish mud,
    Our tempers rising
Among the drifts like the last of the rainbows rising
    Through the remaining hours
Till the sun goes out. What have I done to us?
    I offer these strands,
These unromantic strains, unable to give
    Such royal accompaniment

As horns on the Thames or bronze bells on the Nile
        Or the pipes of goatmen,
But here, the goats themselves in the dying reeds,
        The ringing cows
And bullocks on the banks, pausing to stare
        At our confluence
Along the awkward passage to the bridge
        Over love's divisions.
Landing at nightfall, letting the air run out
        Of what constrained us,
We fold it together, crossing stem to stern,
        Search for our eyes,
And reach ourselves, in time, to wake again
        This music from silence.

Leaving Something Behind

A fox at your neck and snakeskin on your feet,
You have gone to the city behind an ivory brooch,
Wearing your charms for and against desire, bearing your beauty
Past all the gaping doorways, amazing women on edge
And leading men's eyes astray while skirting mayhem,
And I, for a day, must wish you safe in your skin.

The diggers named her the Minnesota Girl. She was fifteen,
Eight thousand years ago, when she drowned in a glacial lake,
Curling to sleep like her sea-snail amulet, holding a turtleshell,
A wolf's tooth, the tine of an antler, carrying somehow
A dozen bones from the feet of water birds. She believed in her charms,
But something found her and kept her. She became what she wore.

She loved her bones and her own husk of creatures
But left them piecemeal on the branching shore.
Without you, fox paws, elephant haunches, all rattling tails,
Snails' feet, turtles' remote hearts, muzzles of wolves,
Stags' ears, and the tongues of water birds are only themselves.
Come safely back. There was nothing in her arms.

Clancy

We bought him at auction, tranquilized to a drooping halt,
A blue-roan burro to be ridden by infants in arms, by tyros
Or the feeblest ladies, to be slapped or curried or manhandled,
A burro for time exposures, an amiable lawnmower.

But he burst out of his delivery truck like a war-horse,
Figure-eighting all night at the end of his swivel chain,
Chin high, octuple-gaited, heehawing through two octaves
Across our field and orchard, over the road, over the river.

While I fenced-in our farm to keep him from barnstorming
Neighbors and dignified horses, then palisaded our house
Like a beleaguered fort, my wife with sugar and rolled oats
And mysteries of her own coaxed him slowly into her favor.

He stood through the muddiest weather, spurning all shelter,
Archenemy of gates and roofs, mangler of halters,
Detector of invisible hackamores, surefooted hoofer
Against the plots of strangers or dogs or the likes of me.

But she would brush him and whisper to him out of earshot
And feed him hazel branches and handfuls of blackberries
And run and prance beside him, while he goated and buck-jumped,
Then stood by the hour with his long soft chin on her shoulder

While I was left on the far side of my own fence
Under the apple trees, playing second pitchfork
Among a scattering of straw over the dark-gold burro-apples
Too powerful for any garden, even the Hesperides.

And I still watch from exile as, night or morning, they wander
Up slope and down without me, neither leading nor following
But simply taking their time over the important pasture,
Considering dew and cobwebs and alfalfa and each other.

And all his ancestors, once booted through mountain passes
Bearing their grubstaked packtrees, or flogged up dusty arroyos
To their bitter ends without water, are grazing now in the bottom
Of her mind and his, digesting this wild good fortune.

Talking Back

This green-and-red, yellow-naped Amazon parrot, Pythagoras,
Is the master of our kitchen table. *Every good boy*
Does fine! he shouts, hanging upside down, and *Pieces of eight*
And gold doubloons! in his cage whose latches he picked with ease
Till we bought a padlock, *To market, to market, to buy a fat pig!*
Home again, home again, and he rings his brass bell, as militant
As salvation, or knocks his trapeze like a punching bag with his beak
Or outfakes and ripostes the treacherous cluster of measuring spoons
Which he pretends are out for his blood. How many times
Have I wished him back in his jungle? Instead, he brings it here
Daily with a voice like sawgrass in raucous counterpoint
To after-work traffic, washing machines, or electric razors
As he jangles back at motors in general, *Who knows*
What evil lurks in the hearts of men? but then, inscrutably,
Refusing to laugh like The Shadow. When he walks on the table
In a fantailed pigeon-toed shuffling strut, getting a taste
Of formica with his leathery tongue, he challenges me
Each morning to fight for my wife if I dare to come near her,
Ruffling his neck and hunching, beak open, his amber eyes
Contracting to malevolent points. I taught him everything
He knows, practically, *Fair and foul are near of kin!*
Including how to love her as he croons in her soft voice,
I'm a green bird, and how to test me for the dialectic hell of it,
What then? sang Plato's ghost, *What then?* as if I knew
The answer which Yeats in his finite wisdom forgot to teach me.

Nine Charms against the Hunter

In the last bar on the way to your wild game,
May the last beer tilt you over among friends
And keep you there till sundown—failing that,
A breakdown on the road, ditching you gently
Where you may hunt for lights and a telephone.
Or may your smell go everywhere through the brush,
Upwind or crosswind. May your feet come down
Invariably crunching loudly on dry sticks.
Or may whatever crosses your hairlines—
The flank of elk or moose, the scut of a deer,
The blurring haunch of a bear, or another hunter
Gaping along his sights at the likes of you—
May they catch you napping or freeze you with buck fever.
Or if you fire, may the stock butting your shoulder
Knock you awake around your bones as you miss,
Or then and there, may the noise pour through your mind
Imaginary deaths to redden your daydreams:
Dazed animals sprawling forward on dead leaves,
Thrashing and kicking, spilling themselves as long
As you could wish, as hard, as game,
And then, if you need it, imaginary skinning,
Plucking of liver and lights, unraveling guts,
Beheading trophies to your heart's content.
Or if these charms have failed and the death is real,
May it fatten you, hour by hour, for the trapped hunter
Whose dull knife beats the inside of your chest.

In the Open Season

By what stretch of the mind had we come there, lurching and crackling
Mile after mile uphill through the ruts and ice-lidded chuckholes
On the logging road, the pine boughs switching across our windows?
It was the middle of gray-green daylight when we stalled, then climbed
On foot into scraggy clearings, while blue and ruffed grouse
Went booming and rocketing slapdash deep under the branches
Beside us, beating our hearts, and the guns began slamming
Their blunt, uninterrupted echoes from valley to valley.
We zigzagged up through the stunted hemlocks, over stumps and snow
Into shale, into light, to a ridgecrest frozen hard as a backbone
And, lying down as if breathing our last, caught the air
One burst at a time. When the world came back, we looked
At dozens of miles of it crumbling away from us
Where bears and deer were spilling out of hiding.
The overlapping thumps of shotgun and rifle
Froze us around each other out of the wind
Where frost had grown on itself, thicker than moss,
In spires and spikelets like a bed of nails
Under our backs by turns. And the light broke out
Of everything we touched in bristling spectrums,
And we felt the day break over again
And again, snow blowing across the sun
To dazzle our half-closed eyes.
But the earth shivered with guns
Below us—the birds, the bears,
And the deer bleeding toward sundown.
We touched each other's wounds
Like star-crossed, stir-crazed lovers
Dying again and again.

Moving into the Garden

Moving into the garden, we settle down
Between the birdbath and the hollyhocks
To wait for the beginning, leaving behind
The house we served for the best years of its life,
Making ourselves at home by the grass spider's
Hollow-throated nest in the ivy.

We have much to learn, such as what to do all day
In the rain that leans the roses against us
And how to follow all night the important paths
Of snails and shy leaf-rollers and lace bugs
And what to make of ourselves among them
At dawn when the cold light touches our fingers

That are no longer thinking of uprooting
Or pruning or transplanting but following
This fall the columbine and bleeding heart
Darkening together, the maidenhair
Closing away like all perennials,
Hardy or delicate, and turning under.

We lift handfuls of earth (is it motherly
Now? was it once? will it be again?)
And wait for the brambles to rise over the slope
Beside us like slow green breakers striking a seawall
To join with us, to mingle with what we love,
With what we've gathered here against the winter.

By the Orchard

Rushing through leaves, they fall
Down, abruptly down
To the ground, bumping the branches,
The windfall apples falling
Yellow into the long grass and lying
Where they have fallen
In the tree's shadow, the shades
Of their soft bruises sinking, opening wide
Mouths to the mouths of creatures
Who like the sun are falling
To flicker, to worm's end under
Themselves, the hatch of moons.

The Fruit of the Tree

With a wall and a ditch between us, I watched the gate-legged dromedary
Creak open from her sleep and come headfirst toward me
As I held out three rust-mottled, tough pears, the color of camels.
When I tossed one, she made no move to catch it; whatever they eat
Lies still and can wait: the roots and sticks, the scrag-ends of brambles.

She straddled, dipping her neck; gray lips and lavender tongue,
Which can choose the best of thorns, thrust the pear to her gullet.
Choking, she mouthed it; her ruminating jaw swung up;
Her eyes lashed out. With a groan she crushed it down,
And ecstasy swept her down into the ditch, till her chin

And her pointed, prolonged face sat on the wall. She stared
At me, inventor and founder of pears. I emptied my sack.
She ate them painfully, clumsy with joy, her withers trembling,
Careless of dust on the bitten and dropped halves, ignoring flies,
Losing herself in the pit of her last stomach.

When she gazed at me again, our mouths were both deserted.
I walked away with myself. She watched me disappear,
Then with a rippling trudge went back to her stable
To snort, to browse on hay, to remember my sack forever.
She'd been used to having no pears, but hadn't known it.

Imagine the hostile runners, the biters of burnooses,
Coughers and spitters, whose legs can kick at amazing angles—
Their single humps would carry us willingly over dunes
Through sandstorms and the swirling jinni to the edges of oases
If they, from their waterless, intractable hearts, might stretch for pears.

Snake Hunt

On sloping, shattered granite, the snake man
From the zoo bent over the half-shaded crannies
Where rattlesnakes take turns out of the sun,
Stared hard, nodded at me, then lunged
With his thick gloves and yanked one up like a root.

And the whole hillside sprang to death with a hissing
Metallic chattering rattle: they came out writhing
In his fists, uncoiling from daydreams,
Pale bellies looping out of darker diamonds
In the shredded sunlight, dropping into his sack.

As I knelt on rocks, my blood went cold as theirs.
One snake coughed up a mouse. I saw what a mouse
Knows, as well as anyone: there, beside me,
In a cleft a foot away from my braced fingers,
Still in its coils, a rattler stirred from sleep.

It moved the wedge of its head back into shadow
And stared at me, harder than I could answer,
Till the gloves came down between us. In the sack,
Like the disembodied muscles of a torso,
It and the others searched among themselves

For the lost good place. I saw them later
Behind plate-glass, wearing their last skins.
They held their venom behind wide-open eyes.

The Death and Resurrection of the Birds

Falling asleep, the birds are falling
Down through the last light's thatchwork farther than rain,
Their grace notes dwindling
Into that downy pit where the first bird
Waits to become them in the nest of the night.

Silent and featherless,
Now they are one dark bird in darkness.

Beginning again, the birds are breaking
Upward, new-fledged at daybreak, their clapping wingbeats
Striking the sides of the sun, the singing brilliant
Dust spun loose on the wind from the end to the beginning.

The Singing Lesson

You must stand erect but at your ease, a posture
Demanding a compromise
Between your spine and your head, your best face forward,
Your willful hands
Not beckoning or clenching or sweeping upward
But drawn in close:
A man with his arms spread wide is asking for it,
A martyred beggar,
A flightless bird on the nest dreaming of flying.
For your full resonance
You must keep your inspiring and expiring moments
Divided but equal,
Not locked like antagonists from breast to throat,
Choking toward silence.

If you have learned, with labor and luck, the measures
You were meant to complete,
You may find yourself before an audience
Singing into the light,
Transforming the air you breathe—that malleable wreckage,
That graveyard of shouts,
That inexhaustible pool of chatter and whimpers—
Into deathless music.
But remember, with your mouth wide open, eyes shut,
Some men will wonder,
When they look at you without listening, whether
You're singing or dying.
Take care to be heard. But even singing alone,
Singing for nothing,
Singing to empty space in no one's honor,
Keep time: it will tell
When you must give the final end-stopped movement
Your tacit approval.

SEQUENCE: TRAVELING LIGHT

Breaking Camp

Having spent a hard-earned sleep, you must break camp in the mountains
At the break of day, pulling up stakes and packing,
Scattering your ashes,
And burying everything human you can't carry. Lifting
Your world now on your shoulders, you should turn
To look back once
At a place as welcoming to a later dead-tired stranger
As it was to your eyes only the other evening,
As the place you've never seen
But must hope for now at the end of a day's rough journey:
You must head for another campsite, maybe no nearer
Wherever you're going
Than where you've already been, but deeply, starkly appealing
Like a lost home: with water, the wind lying down
On a stretch of level earth,
And the makings of a fire to flicker against the night
Which you, traveling light, can't bring along
But must always search for.

Meeting a Bear

If you haven't made noise enough to warn him, singing, shouting,
Or thumping sticks against trees as you walk in the woods,
Giving him time to vanish
(As he wants to) quietly sideways through the nearest thicket,
You may wind up standing face to face with a bear.
Your near future,
Even your distant future, may depend on how he feels
Looking at you, on what he makes of you
And your upright posture
Which, in his world, like a down-swayed head and humped shoulders,
Is a standing offer to fight for territory
And a mate to go with it.
Gaping and staring directly are as risky as running:
To try for dominance or moral authority
Is an empty gesture,
And taking to your heels is an invitation to a dance
Which, from your point of view, will be no circus.
He won't enjoy your smell
Or anything else about you, including your ancestors
Or the shape of your snout. If the feeling's mutual,
It's still out of balance:
He doesn't *care* what you think or calculate; your disapproval
Leaves him as cold as the opinions of salmon.
He may feel free
To act out all his own displeasures with a vengeance:
You would do well to try your meekest behavior,
Standing still
As long as you're not mauled or hugged, your eyes downcast.
But if you must make a stir, do everything sidelong,
Gently and naturally,
Vaguely oblique. Withdraw without turning and start saying
Softly, monotonously, whatever comes to mind
Without special pleading:
Nothing hurt or reproachful to appeal to his better feelings.
He has none, only a harder life than yours.

There's no use singing
National anthems or battle hymns or alma maters
Or any other charming or beastly music.
Use only the dullest,
Blandest, most colorless, undemonstrative speech you can think of,
Bears, for good reason, find it embarrassing
Or at least disarming
And will forget their claws and cover their eyeteeth as an answer.
Meanwhile, move off, yielding the forest floor
As carefully as your honor.

Walking in a Swamp

When you first feel the ground under your feet
Going soft and uncertain,
It's best to start running as fast as you can slog
Even though falling
Forward on your knees and lunging like a cripple.
You may escape completely
Being bogged down in those few scampering seconds.
But if you're caught standing
In deep mud, unable to walk or stagger,
It's time to reconsider
Your favorite postures, textures, and means of moving,
Coming to even terms
With the kind of dirt that won't take no for an answer.
You must lie down now,
Like it or not: if you're in it up to your thighs,
Be seated gently,
Lie back, open your arms, and dream of floating
In a sweet backwater.
Slowly your sunken feet will rise together,
And you may slither
Spread-ottered casually backward out of trouble.
If you stay vertical
And, worse, imagine you're in a fearful struggle,
Trying to swivel
One stuck leg at a time, keeping your body
Above it all,
Immaculate, you'll sink in even deeper,
Becoming an object lesson
For those who wallow after you through the mire,
In which case you should know
For near-future reference: muck is one part water,
One part what-have-you,
Including yourself, now in it over your head,
As upright as ever.

Tracking

The man ahead wasn't expecting you
To follow: he was careless
At first, dislodging stones, not burying ashes,
Forgetting his heelmarks,
Lighting his fires by night to be seen for miles,
Breaking dead silence.
But he's grown wary now: in this empty country
You must learn to read
What you've never read before: the minute language
Of moss and lichen,
The signals of bent grass, the speech of sand,
The gestures of dust.
No man can move two feet from where he is,
Lightfooted or lame,
Without disturbing the natural disorder
Under him always,
And no sly sweeping with branches, no bootless dodging,
No shifting to hardpan,
Not even long excursions across bedrock
Should trick your attention.
If you come to running water, head upstream:
Everything human
Climbs as it runs away and goes to ground later.
What tries to escape you
Will count on you to suffer discouragement,
And so, at dogged last,
If you've shuffled off the deliberate evasions
And not been sidetracked,
Have followed even blind trails, cutting for sign
Through slides and washouts,
You should be prepared for that unwelcome meeting:
The other, staring
Back to see who's made this much of his footprints,
To study your dead-set face
And find out whether you mean to kill him, join him,
Or simply to blunder past.

Missing the Trail

Only a moment ago you were thinking of something
Different, the sky or yesterday or the wind,
But suddenly it's yourself
Alone, strictly alone, having taken a wrong turn
Somewhere behind you, having missed the trail,
Bewildered, now uncertain
Whether to turn back, bear left or right, or flounder ahead
Stubbornly, breaking new ground out of pride or panic,
Or to raise your voice
Out of fear that screaming is the only universal language.
If you come to your senses, all six, taking your time,
The spot where you're standing
Is your best hope. When it first dawns on you you're lost,
You must memorize everything around you, scouring
That place for landmarks,
For rocks, bushes, or trees you'd know again in the dark,
For anything unmistakable to return to,
Or some ragged signal
That can reestablish your eyes, even the shirt off your back,
While you branch out from there, the trunk of your life,
In all directions,
Trying to stumble once more across the vaguest of trails
You may want to follow again for some strange reason
Toward somewhere or other
You may now (having been lost and found) barely remember
Wanting to get to, past the middle of nowhere,
Toward your wit's end.

From Here to There

Though you can see in the distance, outlined precisely
With speechless clarity, the place you must go
The problem remains
Judging how far away you are and getting there safely.
Distant objects often seem close at hand
When looked at grimly,
But between you and those broken hills (so sharply in focus
You have to believe in them with all your senses)
Lies a host of mirages:
Water put out like fire, the shimmer of flying islands,
The unbalancing act of mountains upside down.
Passing through too much air,
Light shifts, fidgets, and veers in ways clearly beyond you,
Confusing its weights and measures with your own
Which are far simpler:
A man on foot can suffer only one guiding principle
Next to his shadow: One Damn Thing After Another,
Meaning his substance
In the shape of his footsoles against the unyielding ground.
When you take a step, whatever you ask to bear you
Is bearing your life:
Sound earth may rest on hollow earth, and stones too solid
To budge in one direction may be ready
To gather no moss
With you, end over end, in another. You've been foolhardy
Enough already to make this slewfooted journey
Through a place without pathways
Where looking back seems as disheartening as relearning
The whole mad lay of the land by heart
After an earthquake.
At last, watching your step, having shrugged off most illusions,
And stumbling close enough to rap your knuckles
Against the reality
Of those unlikely rocks you've stared at through thick and thin
Air and the dumb-shows of light, your hope should be,
As a hardened traveler,

Not to see your trembling hands passing through cloud-stuff,
Some flimsy mock-up of a world spun out of vapor,
But to find yourself
In the Land Behind the Wind where nothing is the matter
But you, brought to your knees, an infirm believer
Asking one more lesson.

Being Shot

You'll hear it split seconds later—the loud afterthought
Booming among tree trunks like a thunder-crack
To startle ravens
And suddenly lift moose-racks dripping with water lilies
For miles around—unless you're too involved,
Too strangely preoccupied
With absorbing the impact of this bullet, in sharp contrast
With your soft flesh and blood, your yielding sinew,
Your tractable bones.
If it hasn't broken your heart or skull, this bit of metal
May strike you as a blunder, a senseless burden,
An appalling intrusion
Into your privacy, to which your body, turning, may take
Vigorous exception, but soon you'll feel it growing
Heavy, then heavier,
And if you haven't fallen involuntarily, you may
Volunteer now and find what ease waits here
On the forest floor,
The duff of sword fern and sorrel, of spike moss and beadruby
That takes without question whatever comes its way,
While you begin to study
At firsthand now the symptoms of shock: the erratic heartbeat,
The unexpected displeasure of half breathing,
The coming of the cold,
The tendency to forget exactly why you're sprawling somewhere
That has slipped your mind for a moment, seeing things
In a new light
Which doesn't come from the sky but from all loose ends
Of all your hopes, your dissolving endeavors
To keep close track
Of who you are, and where you had started from, and why
You were walking in the woods before this stranger
(Who is leaning over you
Now with a disarming smile) interfered so harshly.
Not wishing to make yourself conspicuous
By your endless absence

And having meant no harm by moving quietly, searching
Among this second growth of your own nature
For its first wildness,
You may offer him your empty hands, now red as his hat,
And he may grant mercy or, on the other hand,
Give you as gracefully
As time permits, as lack of witnesses will allow
Or your punctured integrity will stand for,
A graceful coup de grace.

Waiting in a Rain Forest

The rain does not fall here: it stands in the air around you
Always, drifting from time to time like breath
And gathering on the leaflike
Pale shield lichen as clearly as the intricate channels
Along the bloodwort gleaming like moths' eyes,
Out of the maidenhair
And the running pine and the soft small towers of club moss
Where you must rest now under a green sky
In a land without flowers
Where the wind has fixed its roots and the motionless weather
Leaves you with nothing to do but watch the unbroken
Promises of the earth
And know whatever lies down, like you or a fallen nurse-log,
Will taste the deepest longing of young hemlocks
And learn without fear or favor
This gentlest of undertakings: moss mending your ways
While many spring from one to a wild garden
Flourishing in silence.

Traveling Light

Through this most difficult country, this world we had known
As a cross-grained hummocky bog-strewn jumble of brambles
Stretching through summer,
We find after blizzard and sunlight, traveling in the winter,
A rolling parkland under our snowshoes
Where every color
Has drifted out of our shadows into a brittle whiteness.
And so we begin shuffling our way forward
Above the invisible
Deadfalls and pitfallen brush, above the deeply buried
Landmarks and blazes we had found misleading,
Above the distraction
Of flowers and sweet berries and birdsongs that held us
Back, breathing and tasting, sitting, listening.
Now we are hurrying
With the smooth swift scuttling of webs, our feet not touching
The earth, our breath congealing, our ears hearing
More than we can believe in
In the denser air: disembodied by the cold, the shouting,
Shouting from miles away, the slamming of gunfire,
The ghosts of axes.
But, by tonight, we must learn the serious art of sleeping,
Of lying down, not going on nerve alone
To court exhaustion
Which, here in the deep snow, is another name for forever.
We will make fire, then turn in each other's arms,
Embracing once more
All we have brought this far in our rawhided fiber,
By rock, by river, by ourselves under the branches
Of this living fir tree
Where, unlike us, the grouse may perch through a whole winter.
And then the cold-spelled morning will make us stare
Into each other's eyes
For the first signs of whiteness, stare at the ends of fingers,
Then into the distance where the whitening
Marks the beginning

Of the place we were always looking for: so full of light,
So full of flying light, it is all feathers
Which we must wear
As we had dreamed we would, not putting frostbitten hands
Into the freshly slaughtered breasts of birds
But snowblindly reaching
Into this dazzling whiteout, finding where we began,
Not naming the wonder yet but remembering
The simply amazing
World of our first selves where believing is once more seeing
The cold speech of the earth in the colder air
And knowing it by heart.

After Consulting My Yellow Pages

All went well today in the barbers' college:
The razor handles pointed gracefully outward,
The clippers were singing like locusts. And far away
On the fox farms, the red and silver sun brushed lightly
Tail after tail. Happily, the surveyors
Measured the downhill pasture through a theodolite,
Untroubled by birch trees. The makers of fraternal regalia
Conceived a new star-burst, and the parakeet
In the green bird hospital was coaxed out of danger.
Business came flying out of the horse-meat market,
And under the skillful world, the conduits groped
Forward, heavy with wires, to branch at the lake.
Fish brokers prodded salmon on the walloping dock.
The manifold continuous forms and the luminous products
Emerged, endlessly shining, while the cooling towers
Poured water over themselves like elephants.
Busily the deft hands of the locksmith and wig-maker
In basement and loft, in the magnifying light,
Turned at their labors. The universal joints,
Hose-couplings, elastic hosiery, shingles and shakes,
The well-beloved escrow companies, the heat-exchangers,
Bead-stringers, makers of disappearing beds,
The air-compressors randy with oxygen—
All sprang, remarkably, out of the swinging doors.

And where were you? What did you do today?

The Labors of Thor

Stiff as the icicles in their beards, the Ice Kings
Sat in the great cold hall and stared at Thor
Who had lumbered this far north to stagger them
With his gifts, which (back at home) seemed scarcely human.

"Immodesty forbids," his sideman Loki
Proclaimed throughout the preliminary bragging
And reeled off Thor's accomplishments, fit for Sagas
Or a seat on the bench of the gods. With a sliver of beard

An Ice King picked his teeth: "Is he a drinker?"
And Loki boasted of challengers laid out
As cold as pickled herring. The Ice King offered
A horn-cup long as a harp's neck, full of mead.

Thor braced himself for elbow and belly room
And tipped the cup and drank as deep as mackerel,
Then deeper, reaching down for the halibut
Till his broad belt buckled. He had quaffed one inch.

"Maybe he's better at something else," an Ice King
Muttered, yawning. Remembering the boulders
He'd seen Thor heave and toss in the pitch of anger,
Loki proposed a bout of lifting weights.

"You men have been humping rocks from here to there
For ages," an Ice King said. "They cut no ice.
Lift something harder." And he whistled out
A gray-green cat with cold, mouse-holey eyes.

Thor gave it a pat, then thrust both heavy hands
Under it, stooped and heisted, heisted again,
Turned red in the face and bit his lip and heisted
From the bottom of his heart—and lifted one limp forepaw.

Now pink in the face himself, Loki said quickly
That heroes can have bad days, like bards and beggars,
But Thor of all mortals was the grossest wrestler
And would stake his demigodhood on one fall.

Seeming too bored to bother, an Ice King waved
His chilly fingers around the mead-hall, saying,
"Does anyone need some trifling exercise
Before we go glacier-calving in the morning?"

An old crone hobbled in, foul-faced and gamy,
As bent in the back as any bitch of burden,
As gray as water, as feeble as an oyster.
An Ice King said, "She's thrown some boys in her time."

Thor would have left, insulted, but Loki whispered,
"When the word gets south, she'll be at least an ogress."
Thor reached out sullenly and grabbed her elbow,
But she quicksilvered him and grinned her gums.

Thor tried his patented hammerlock takedown,
But she melted away like steam from a leaky sauna.
He tried a whole Nelson: it shrank to half, to a quarter,
Then nothing. He stood there, panting at the ceiling,

"Who got me into this demigoddiness?"
As flashy as lightning, the woman belted him
With her bony fist and boomed him to one knee,
But fell to a knee herself, as pale as moonlight.

Bawling for shame, Thor left by the back door,
Refusing to be consoled by Loki's plans
For a quick revision of the Northodox Version
Of the evening's deeds, including Thor's translation

From vulnerable flesh and sinew into a dish
Fit for the gods and a full apotheosis
With catches and special effects by the sharpest gleemen
Available in an otherwise flat season.

He went back south, tasting his bitter lesson
Moment by moment for the rest of his life,
Believing himself a pushover faking greatness
Along a tawdry strain of misadventures.

Meanwhile, the Ice Kings trembled in their chairs
But not from the cold: they'd seen a man hoist high
The Great Horn-Cup that ends deep in the ocean
And lower all Seven Seas by his own stature;

They'd seen him budge the Cat of the World and heft
The pillar of one paw, the whole north corner;
They'd seen a mere man wrestle with Death herself
And match her knee for knee, grunting like thunder.

This Is a Wonderful Poem

Come at it carefully, don't trust it, that isn't its right name,
It's wearing stolen rags, it's never been washed, its breath
Would look moss-green if it were really breathing,
It won't get out of the way, it stares at you
Out of eyes burnt gray as the sidewalk,
Its skin is overcast with colorless dirt,
It has no distinguishing marks, no I.D. cards,
It wants something of yours but hasn't decided
Whether to ask for it or just take it,
There are no policemen, no friendly neighbors,
No peacekeeping busybodies to yell for, only this
Thing standing between you and the place you were headed,
You have about thirty seconds to get past it, around it,
Or simply to back away and try to forget it,
It won't take no for an answer: try hitting it first
And you'll learn what's trembling in its torn pocket.
Now, what do you want to do about it?

The Shooting of John Dillinger Outside the Biograph Theater, July 22, 1934

Chicago ran a fever of a hundred and one that groggy Sunday.
A reporter fried an egg on a sidewalk; the air looked shaky.
And a hundred thousand people were in the lake like shirts in a laundry.
Why was Johnny lonely?
Not because two dozen solid citizens, heat-struck, had keeled over
    backward.
Not because those lawful souls had fallen out of their sockets and melted.
But because the sun went down like a lump in a furnace or a bull in the
    Stockyards.
Where was Johnny headed?
Under the Biograph Theater sign that said, "Our Air Is Refrigerated."
Past seventeen FBI men and four policemen who stood in doorways and
    sweated.
Johnny sat down in a cold seat to watch Clark Gable get electrocuted.
Had Johnny been mistreated?
Yes, but Gable told the D.A. he'd rather fry than be shut up forever.
Two women sat by Johnny. One looked sweet, one looked like J. Edgar
    Hoover.
Polly Hamilton made him feel hot, but Anna Sage made him shiver.
Was Johnny a good lover?
Yes, but he passed out his share of squeezes and pokes like a jittery
    masher
While Agent Purvis sneaked up and down the aisle like an extra usher,
Trying to make sure they wouldn't slip out till the show was over.
Was Johnny a four-flusher?
No, not if he knew the game. He got it up or got it back.
But he liked to take snapshots of policemen with his own Kodak,
And once in a while he liked to take them with an automatic.
Why was Johnny frantic?
Because he couldn't take a walk or sit down in a movie
Without being afraid he'd run smack into somebody
Who'd point at his rearranged face and holler, "Johnny!"
Was Johnny ugly?
Yes, because Dr. Wilhelm Loeser had given him a new profile
With a baggy jawline and squint eyes and an erased dimple,
With kangaroo-tendon cheekbones and a gigolo's mustache that
    should've been illegal.

Did Johnny love a girl?
Yes, a good-looking, hard-headed Indian named Billie Frechette.
He wanted to marry her and lie down and try to get over it,
But she was locked in jail for giving him first aid and comfort.
Did Johnny feel hurt?
He felt like breaking a bank or jumping over a railing
Into some panicky teller's cage to shout, "Reach for the ceiling!"
Or like kicking some vice president in the bum checks and smiling.
What was he really doing?
Going up the aisle with the crowd and into the lobby
With Polly saying, "Would *you* do what Clark done?" And Johnny saying,
    "Maybe."
And Anna saying, "If he'd been smart, he'd of acted like Bing Crosby."
Did Johnny look flashy?
Yes, his white-on-white shirt and tie were luminous.
His trousers were creased like knives to the tops of his shoes,
And his yellow straw hat came down to his dark glasses.
Was Johnny suspicious?
Yes, and when Agent Purvis signaled with a trembling cigar,
Johnny ducked left and ran out of the theater,
And innocent Polly and squealing Anna were left nowhere.
Was Johnny a fast runner?
No, but he crouched and scurried past a friendly liquor store
Under the coupled arms of double-daters, under awnings, under stars,
To the curb at the mouth of an alley. He hunched there.
Was Johnny a thinker?
No, but he was thinking more or less of Billie Frechette
Who was lost in prison for longer than he could possibly wait,
And then it was suddenly too hard to think around a bullet.
Did anyone shoot straight?
Yes, but Mrs. Etta Natalsky fell out from under her picture hat.
Theresa Paulus sprawled on the sidewalk, clutching her left foot.
And both of them groaned loud and long under the streetlight.
Did Johnny like that?
No, but he lay down with those strange women, his face in the alley,
One shoe off, cinders in his mouth, his eyelids heavy.
When they shouted questions at him, he talked back to nobody.
Did Johnny lie easy?
Yes, holding his gun and holding his breath as a last trick,
He waited, but when the agents came close, his breath wouldn't work.

Clark Gable walked his last mile; Johnny ran half a block.
Did he run out of luck?
Yes, before he was cool, they had him spread out on dished-in marble
In the Cook County Morgue, surrounded by babbling people
With a crime reporter presiding over the head of the table.
Did Johnny have a soul?
Yes, and it was climbing his slippery windpipe like a trapped burglar.
It was beating the inside of his ribcage, hollering, "Let me out of here!"
Maybe it got out, and maybe it just stayed there.
Was Johnny a money-maker?
Yes, and thousands paid 25¢ to see him, mostly women,
And one said, "I wouldn't have come, except he's a moral lesson,"
And another, "I'm disappointed. He feels like a dead man."
Did Johnny have a brain?
Yes, and it always worked best through the worst of dangers,
Through flatfooted hammerlocks, through guarded doors, around
      corners,
But it got taken out in the morgue and sold to some doctors.
Could Johnny take orders?
No, but he stayed in the wicker basket carried by six men
Through the bulging crowd to the hearse and let himself be locked in,
And he stayed put as it went driving south in a driving rain.
And he didn't get stolen?
No, not even after his old hard-nosed dad refused to sell
The quick-drawing corpse for $10,000 to somebody in a carnival.
He figured he'd let *Johnny* decide how to get to Hell.
Did anyone wish him well?
Yes, half of Indiana camped in the family pasture,
And the minister said, "With luck, he could have been a minister."
And up the sleeve of his oversized gray suit, Johnny twitched a finger.
Does anyone remember?
Everyone still alive. And some dead ones. It was a new kind of holiday
With hot and cold drinks and hot and cold tears. They planted him in a
      cemetery
With three unknown vice presidents, Benjamin Harrison, and James
      Whitcomb Riley,
Who never held up anybody.

The Burglar

Being a burglar, you slip out of doors in the morning
And look at the street by looking at the sky,
Not being taken in by anything blue.
You must look to the left or right to see across.
If nothing strikes your eye, if no one comes running,
You've stolen another day.

You must spend it on your toes
At the edges of buildings, doorways, and windows
Wherever no one is watching close enough.
Keep your fingers light as smoke.
You may have permission to kiss with one eye open.
Try every door while leaning away from it.

But sundown is serious; it's time to go home
To the house that will draw you under its empty wing.
Climbing like ivy up the drains, go through
The farthest window into a dark room.
Wait there to hear how everything has gone.
Then, masking every motion,

Glide to the stairwell.
They will be eating dinner: the man and the woman
At opposite ends of a white and silver table;
Between them, food and candles and children.
Their knives and forks go in and out of their mouths;
Whatever they do will aim them toward each other.

Now, follow your fingerprints around all corners
From nightlatch to velvet lid, from hasp to stone.
Everything locked, of course, has been locked for you:
You must break in softly, take whatever you find
Whether you understand what it is or not.
Breathe in, reach out,

Stealing one thing at a time.
If you grow hungry, thinking of their desserts,
It's time to vanish over the windowsill.
You must go without their dinner into the night,
Not saying good-bye, not waiting to scrawl a note
To say you're running away, but running away.

The Holdup

First comes a fence, then the mouth of an alley,
Then a shadow on the other side of shadows
Becomes a pole, a doorway, a garbage can
Becoming a bush with a voice becoming an arm
Holding a gun at my back. This is a hold-up.
We wait a moment. We listen
For whatever it might be I'm going to say.
The wind crawls out from under the parked cars.

My arms go up in the air. My hands turn white.
Apparently I won't be saying anything.
He empties the deep pocket over my heart,
Then pats my hips as if guessing my weight.
Half-turning, I see the stocking down his face
Erasing lips and eyes, smoothing his nose.
We pass the time of night together.
He does the breathing for both of us.

The muzzle touches my back
Gently, like the muzzle of a dog. What's holding me up?
Take off your shoes. I stand in stocking feet
On the cinders. He begins to fade.
I had been walking from streetlight to streetlight,
My shadow straight as a footbridge under me,
Forgetting the mouths of alleys by moonlight.
My shoes and my money are running away in the dark.

The Visiting Hour

Strip off your clothes and give them to a man
In a uniform, hurry to take a shower,
Put on a starchy, stark-white coverall
That can stand up by itself, then keeping in line,
March to the visitor's room.

It has lamps, rugs, curtains, movable furniture,
And a woman among some women, looking at you
And wearing a dress and holding out her arms
(Which may be entered against her)
And shutting and opening her mouth for an hour.

Standing behind his bullet-proof glass, the guard
Has been instructed to stare, but stares at the wall,
The ceiling, or between your bodies
As if recalling games on television.
What you can do is act like him for her:

Your eyes must look at something common between you—
A crack, a flower on a cushion.
Your hands may touch each other item by item
In order, checking down the list of reminders.
You may reach for almost anything but conclusions.

When a bell rings, there is nothing left to answer,
No one is calling or waiting, nothing is ready—
The time has simply gone, and the time has come
To say good-bye like scouts of opposing factions
From opposite closing doors.

From the corridor, you'll enter an empty room
To be stripped and searched for imaginary objects:
Stooping, squatting, and squinting, the guards go through
Your closets and blind alleys
To catch you keeping what you can never get.

The long way back will take you past a gate
Where you can see a man outside in a tower.
His searchlight, his eyes, his rifle
All turn toward you if you stop to wave.
He must know you to let you out. He doesn't know you.

And in Cell Block D, nobody wants to shoot you.
Those tiers with railings
Rise forty feet like the face of a motel
With ice on every floor. Like venetian blinds,
The catwalks show you mounting, kneeling, or lying.

The guards in the gallery simply look and listen
Over their sights if you thumb your nose or scream
Or try to throw something far enough to reach them.
They'll put your name on a list; then visitors
Will have to imagine you for years and years.

The Night of the Sad Women

They are undressing slowly by closed doors,
Unable to find themselves, fading in mirrors
And feeling faint, finding their eyes in time
But seeing, instead, the rooms behind their shoulders

Where nothing is going to work, where photographs
Stand still in frames, arresting other days
When things were turning out. Now turning in,
They are lowering shades and turning off the lights,

But find their fingers lighter than pale linen
At the sinking bedside, seeing their own hands
In front of their faces wavering like gauze,
Then edging away to search in fallen purses.

But they lose touch. In the middle of their rooms
The night begins, the night of the loose threads
Which hang like spiders' lifelines out of seams
To be raveled to the floor, but not to end.

At St. Vincent DePaul's

"Free shoes, help yourself"

Buckling their thin soles,
These squads of shoes
In lines under the rain
Are shining this morning,
Rocking on round heels
Or turning up at the toes
As if to jump for joy
Or jump out of the way:
Oxfords and safety shoes
And boots whose arches fell
Flatter than handprints
Are warping back to life,
The cracked and wrinkled hides
As supple as fishskins
Now in the falling water
Under their own steam
Like the rising ghosts of socks,
The sneakers stuck together,
Slippers whose pompons
Bloom like anemones,
Golf shoes for trespassing,
The tongueless, the mismatched
For an hour helping themselves,
Free as long as they last.

Bums at Breakfast

Daily, the bums sat down to eat in our kitchen.
They seemed to be whatever the day was like:
If it was hot or cold, they were hot or cold;
If it was wet, they came in dripping wet.
One left his snowy shoes on the back porch
But his socks stuck to the clean linoleum,
And one, when my mother led him to the sink,
Wrung out his hat instead of washing his hands.

My father said they'd made a mark on the house,
A hobo's sign on the sidewalk, pointing the way.
I hunted everywhere, but never found it.
It must have said, "It's only good in the morning—
When the husband's out." My father knew by heart
Lectures on Thrift and Doggedness,
But he was always either working or sleeping.
My mother didn't know any advice.

They ate their food politely, with old hands,
Not looking around, and spoke in short, plain answers.
Sometimes they said what they'd been doing lately
Or told us what was wrong; but listening hard,
I broke their language into secret codes:
Their *east* meant *west*, their *job* meant *walking and walking*,
Their *money* meant *danger*, *home* meant *running and hiding*,
Their *father* and *mother* were different kinds of weather.

Dumbly, I watched them leave by the back door,
Their pockets empty as a ten-year-old's;
Yet they looked twice as rich, being full of breakfast.
I carried mine like a lump all the way to school.
When I was growing hungry, where would they be?
None ever came twice. Never to lunch or dinner.
They were always starting fresh in the fresh morning.
I dreamed of days that stopped at the beginning.

A Valedictory to Standard Oil of Indiana

In the darkness east of Chicago, the sky burns over the plumbers'
   nightmares
Red and blue, and my hometown lies there loaded with gasoline.
Registers ring like gas pumps, pumps like pinballs, pinballs like broken
   alarm clocks,
And it's time for morning, but nothing's going to work.
From cat-cracker to candle-shop, from grease-works along the pipeline,
Over storage tanks like kings on a checkerboard ready to jump the county,
The word goes out: With refined regrets
We suggest you sleep all day in your houses shaped like lunch buckets
And don't show up at the automated gates.
Something else will tap the gauges without yawning
And check the valves at the feet of the cooling towers without complaining.
Standard Oil is canning my high school classmates
And the ones who fell out of junior high or slipped in the grades.
What should they do, gassed up in their Tempests and Comets, raring to go
Somewhere with their wives scowling in front and kids stuffed in the back,
Past drive-ins jammed like car lots, trying to find the beaches
But blocked by freights for hours, stopped dead in their tracks
Where the rails, as thick as thieves along the lakefront,
Lower their crossing gates to shut the frontier? What can they think about
As they stare at the sides of boxcars for a sign,
And Lake Michigan drains slowly into Lake Huron,
The mills level the Dunes, and the eels go sailing through the trout,
And mosquitoes inherit the evening, while toads no bigger than horseflies
Hop crazily after them over the lawns and sidewalks, and the rainbows fall
Flat in the oil they came from? There are two towns now,
One dark, one going to be dark, divided by Cyclone fences:
One pampered and cared for like pillboxes and cathedrals,
The other vanishing overnight in the dumps and swamps like a struck
   sideshow.
As the Laureate of the Class of '44—which doesn't know it has one—
I offer this poem, not from hustings or barricades
Or the rickety stage where George Rogers Clark stood glued to the wall,
But from another way out, like Barnum's "This Way to the Egress,"
Which moved the suckers when they'd seen enough. Get out of town.

A Touch of the Mother

She stands in the hallway, waiting for a sign
Of breath or smoke, but nothing squeaks the floor
Or whispers at the sink or drifts through transoms.
She has shut the house for the night, but not her eyes:

She threads them up the stairs like the eyes of needles,
Taking a stitch or two, but not in time:
This is the time when all her basting ravels,
When hooks slip out of eyes, and seams come open.

She goes to bed like all good girls and boys
And sisters and husbands by the hands of clocks,
Whether or not those hands will hold her off
Or turn her in or turn her luminous.

Now she must stir her life until it's smooth,
Folding the beaten whiteness through and through
Her mind, like a level cupful taking its place
With all the rich ingredients of the night,

But something chills her. The layers of her dream
Sink in the middle, stiffen, and turn cold:
What is it? Shut the door, the delivery men
Come slouching and lounging into her preserves,

And first you must wash them clean with homemade soap,
Caress them, dry them gently with a towel,
Then soak them for hours in wormwood and witch hazel,
They will fall off and give you no more trouble,

And after turning thick at a rolling boil,
They must form a ball when you drop them in cold water,
Screw the lids hard and store them upside down
In your dark cellar, they will last forever,

And now you know the measure of everything:
Your hand is half as wide as it is long,
Around your wrist is half around your neck,
And twice around your neck is around your waist,

And the cows come back for the leather in your shoes,
The sheep come back for the wool in the tossing blankets,
The geese come back for the feathers in the pillow,
And something blue goes in and out the window.

Elegy for a Woman Who Remembered Everything

She knew the grades of all her neighbors' children, the birthdays
Of cousins once removed, the addresses of friends who had moved
Once at least—to the coordinates of cemeteries
Where their choice views lay over their front feet.

If it had a name or a number, she missed nothing:
A mailman's neck size, the unpronounceable village where the dentist's
Wife's half-sister ruined her kneecap, an almanac of sutures,
The ingredients of five thousand immemorial crocks.

Her ears were as perfectly pitched as a piano tuner's.
In the maze of total recall, she met with amazement
The data of each new day, absorbed the absorbing facts and the absorbent
Fictions of everyone's life but her own, losing the thread

Of that thin tracery in dialogue hauled back verbatim
Through years leaning cracked and crooked against each other.
Death, you may dictate as rapidly or incoherently as you wish:
She will remember everything about you. Nothing will escape her.

For a Man Who Died in His Sleep

Once in, he can stay as long as he remembers
To lock the door behind him, being afraid
Of nothing within the ordinary passage
Where he hangs his hat and coat, thinking of bed.

He feels as safe as houses: the predictable ceiling,
The floor at its level best, the walls, the windows
Beyond which the sky, under glass, is slowly streaming
Harmlessly westward with its tricks and shadows,

And going upstairs, he lies down to be soft
In a nest of boxes fitted against the night.
He shuts his lids like theirs and, wrapped like a gift,
Presents himself to sleep, to be opened by daylight.

At first, there is nothing, then something, then everything
Under the doors and over the windowsills
And down the chimney, through the foundation, crawling
From jamb to joist and muttering in the walls,

And he lies tongue-tied under the gaping roof
Through which the weather pours the news of his death:
In sheets and lightning, the broken end of his life
Comes pouring crownfire through the roof of his mouth,

And now he dreams he is dreaming that he knows
His heart's in the right place, safe, beating for good
Against the beams and braces of his house
All the good nights to follow, knocking on wood.

Doors

All over town at the first rattle of night
The doors go shut,
Flat hasp over iron staple, bolt into strike,
Or latch into groove;
And locked and double-locked and burglar-chained,
All of them wait
For the worst, or for morning, steady in their frames:
From hinge to lock stile,
From hard head-casing down to the plinth block,
The doors hang still,
One side for knocking and one for hiding away,
One side for love
And one for crying out loud in the long night
To the pounding heart.

Out for a Night

It was No, no, no, practicing at a chair,
And No at the wall, and one for the fireplace,
And down the stairs it was No over the railing,
And two for the dirt, and three Noes for the air,

And four in a row rapidly over the bar,
Becoming Maybe, Maybe, from spittoon to mirror,
It was shrugging cheeks on one face after another,
And Perhaps and So-So at both ends of a cigar,

Five, and it was Yes as a matter of fact
Who said it wasn't all the way down the bottle,
It was Hell Yes over and lightly underfoot,
And tongue like a welcome mat for the bartender,

And Yes in the teeth, Yes like a cracked whistle,
And one for you, and two for the rest of us,
Indeed, Indeed, the chair got up on the table,
And Yes up on the chair and kissed the light

And the light burned, and Yes fell out of the chair,
And the chair slid off the table, and it was Maybe
All over the floor, tilted, it was squat,
And plunge to the rear, and smack lips like a baby,

It was five for the fingers Absolutely,
Four in the corners, it was three for the show,
And two descending eyebrows to make a ceiling,
And No to the knees and chin, and one Good-bye.

Closing Time

At midnight, flaking down like chromium
Inside the tavern, light slips off the bar
And tumbles in our laps. The tumbler falling
Off the edge of the table goes to pieces
As quick as mercury around our shoes.
Good night to shuffleboard and counter-check.
The last ball bearing pins its magnet down
And sinks into a socket like the moon.

Over the rings around our eyes, the clock
Says time to decipher wives, husbands, and cars
On keychains swinging under bleary light.
Good night to folding friends on the parking lot
As parallel as windows in a wallet.
Lined up like empties on the curb, good night
To all who make the far side of the street,
Their eyelids pressed as tight as bottlecaps.

Good night to those with jacks as openers,
Those whose half-cases chill their pelvises,
And those with nothing on tap all day tomorrow
Who wind up sleeping somewhere cold as stars,
Who make the stairs and landings, but not doors,
Those in the tubs, or hung on banisters,
Those with incinerators in their arms,
Whose mouths lie open for another one.

Good night to drivers driven by themselves
To curve through light years at the straightaway.
Good night to cloverleaf and yellow-streak,
To all those leading sheriff's deputies
Over soft shoulders into power poles,
The red-in-the-face whose teeth hang down by nerves,
The far-afield, the breakers of new ground
Who cartwheel out of sight, end over end.

Free Passage

Come away, my sea-lane baggage,
For a crack at the sky.
Come with me in an armlock over the ocean, my china breakage,
We shall go everywhere in a day, grant liberty, squeak, and never die.

From docks to lavender palaces,
Oh what comings and goings, my rattan May basket!
Adored as we fall through tissue paper, through balconies, fountains, and
    trellises,
We shall be borne up like desserts in cream, stuffed like a brisket,

And spun in the air like platters.
At concerts, we shall arrive in all three aisles at once, be lionized in
    jungles, horsed at the seaside.
Chairmen on tiptoe and the giddy, sidelong doctors
Will toast us and be irrevocably toasted.

I have initialed everything, bought floating flashlights,
Filled my binocular flasks with the hottest chutney.
Bye, Mommy! Bye, Daddy! Bye, Sissy! Bye-bye, Fatso!
I'm salting off on the briny with my candy.

Oh my snifter, my tumble-rick, sweet crank of the stars,
My banjo-bottomed, fretful girl,
Tear off those swatches of silk, your hems and haws, and coil them up like
    streamers—
Get set to toss them over the bounding rail.

Sal volatile! Coral uplift! Oh my pink receiver! Freely I swear
Our tanglefoot Rosicrucian wedding on a gangplank, among the hoots
    and the spouting fireboats,
Above flashbulbs, fish heads, and the drowning divers,
Will be as immortal as rats.

A Day in the City

Dismounting from stools and benches, pouring through bars,
Let's do the day up brown,
Knock it back like a short drink, get off our trolley,
Put our foot downtown.

There, cutting the sun in half with our eyelids,
Sinister with love,
We shall wait till those feet, swollen to thousands on the pavement,
Are aching to move.

Then from the joints at our knees, the crooks at our elbows,
From all the hugging sides,
Through the calves and hams, the perpendicular marches
Will drill us into squads.

Rising from cornerstones, cripples with bristling pencils
Will jam on their caps
And join us—the floorwalkers and shoplifters, gulls and barkers,
The blind men in their cups,

And the churruping children, the sailors and loaded Indians,
Fur-bearing stylish stouts,
All thronging from broken curb to curb and up the lampposts,
Onto ledges like goats.

And the city is ours. See, the bridges all give up, the arcades
Rattle their silver shops,
Buildings chip in, the sidewalks roll over like dogs, hotels
Chime their fire escapes.

Here on a glittering carpet of plate glass go dancing
Till leggings and bandages
Trail us like trains round the fountain to the plaza, till our faces
Leap from our jaws,

And our sleeves roll back to the trombones and armbands,
And, shooting the mailchutes,
We stand in circles on every floor, shaking our palms,
Flagging our bedsheets.

We shall trump up a total noise, a silence battered
Like rams in the air.
Let the sewers hoot, all risers drop their treads
To the wrenched foot of the stair.

Then quietly, left and right, with our bandoliers
Crossed on our blouses,
We shall drift away through the empty business ends of the streets
To go back to pieces,

While the city lets out the fiery-red, grumbling water wagons
To lay the dust,
And sends toward our houses, through every alley,
The huge, defaced,

Skulking, familiar, handle-breaking, off-key garbagemen
Who had been killed,
But who now heap under the raised lids, our old lives
Before they are cold.

The Apotheosis of the Garbagemen

And they come back in the night through alleys to find us
By the clashing of raised lids,
By garage doors' lifted heads, the swung gates, the bottomless
Galvanized cans on their shoulders,
In luminous coveralls
They follow the easy directions on boxes, scattering
Bushels of brown grass and apple cores,
Old candy wrappers folded around sweet nothings,
And sacks with their stains on fire,
They are coming through hedges, dragging geometry
In a dark clutch of rainbows,
See, the smashed jars
Prinked out with light, and the vacuum bags
Bursting their dust in the night like the phantasms of horseflies,
Through the burning bacon fat
Their baseball caps go flying, their feet
As solid as six-packs on the lawn, the slam-bang of their coming
Sending the lettuce leaves against our windows
Like luna moths, the marrow whistling
Out of the wishbones of turkeys, the husks and rinds,
The lost-wax castings of corncobs and teabags,
The burnt-out lightbulbs pulsing in midair,
The coupons filled out
With our last names for all the startling offers,
Oh see, their hands are lifted by the gloves
Untying the knots in plastic bags, to catch
The half-burnt ashes raining around their heads,
The crusts and empties.
As the skeletons of lampshades catch at the first light,
They are going back in their empty trucks and singing
To the dump, to the steaming rust
In the rolling, hunch-backed, beckoning earth,
The sea of decay where our foundering fathers
Rubbled their lives,

They have found the way
Back to God's plenty, to rags and riches,
But will come back to us with all we could wish for
In the darkness, singing love and wild appetite,
The good rats and roaches,
The beautiful hogs and billygoats dancing around them.

To My Friend Whose Parachute Did Not Open

Thrown backward first, head over heels in the wind
Like solid streamers from the wing to tail,
You counted whatever pulses came to mind—
The black, the bright—and at the third, you pulled,
Pulled savagely at the ring clenched in your hand.

Down the smooth slope of your trajectory,
Obeying physics like a bauble of hail,
Thirty-two feet per second per second hurled
Toward treetops, cows, and crouching gravity
From the unreasonable center of the world,

You saw the cords trail out from behind your back,
Rise up and stand, tied to a piece of cloth
Whose edges wobbled, but would not spread wide
To borrow a cup of air and hold you both.
O that tall shimmer whispered you were dead.

You outraced thought. What good was thinking then?
Poor time—no time for plunging into luck
Which had, like your whirling, weightless flesh, grown thin.
I know angelic wisdom leaped from your mouth,
But not in words, for words can be afraid:

You sang a paean at the speed of sound,
Compressed miraculous air within your head
And made it fountain upward like a cowl.
And if you didn't, then you struck the ground.
And if you struck the ground, both of us died.

Speech from a Comedy

Scene: The wreckage of Heaven

I am God. But all my creatures are unkind to me.
They think of themselves. Why don't they think of me?
I'm holier than they.
         Chorus   God is lovely.
If I descended and rode through the streets,
Would they take off their hats?
No, they'd keep their hands in each other's pockets.
         Chorus   God is out of sorts.
Or if I showed up to give a formal address
Including an enormous amount of sound, godly advice,
They'd turn and wriggle away like a school of fish.
         Chorus   God is endless.
I burned myself in a bush once. Day and night,
I burned like a pillar of virtue in the desert.
I even let them watch me ride in my chariot.
         Chorus   God is great.
I gave them Aaron's rod when they were on the rocks.
I plagued their enemies with a thousand dirty tricks.
I let them burn rams in thickets instead of their precious Isaacs.
         Chorus   God is on their backs.
When things looked so black they couldn't tell his from hers,
I parted the waters,
Saving a few. But drowning a lot of others.
         Chorus   God is feeling worse.
Didn't I die for them?
Hang myself? And shed the Blood of the Lamb?
What more could I do? Try it yourself sometime.
         Chorus   God is sublime.
Now they forsake me. Leave me up in the air.
Sinning. Thinking of pleasure.
The more I leave them alone, the worse they are.
         Chorus   God is pure.
They lie all night in their houses stacked in rows,
Their knees pulled up, their heads stuffed into pillows,
Imagining new ways to break my laws.
         Chorus   God is jealous.

When I show them a bad example, plastered and confused,
Chances are he'll be headlined and idolized.
The only law of mine they like is getting circumcised.
        Chorus   God is not amused.
I didn't ask for anything impossible.
I said, "Love me—and not just once in a while."
But all men were created fickle.
        Chorus   God is immortal.
I'll settle with Everyman.
I had his dinner all laid out in my mansion,
But *he* had to try cooking his *own*.
        Chorus   God is burning.
Just because angels are blasé and neuter,
Did he think I'd be contented forever and ever
Playing with Ezekiel's wheel or climbing up and down Jacob's ladder?
        Chorus   God is boiling over.
I made him in my image, didn't I?
I gave him my tooth for a tooth, my eye for an eye.
How could I turn out such an unreasonable facsimile?
        Chorus   God is mighty sorry.
He'll be made to see the way things really are.
If he's so fond of slaughter,
I can get it for him wholesale just by losing my temper.
        Chorus   God's a man-of-war.
I might have shown him mercy,
But nobody asked me.
The best things in Heaven are costly.
        Chorus   God is free.
All right, he's dug his bed. Now let him lie in it
A thousand years at a stretch on a strict diet
While worms with their noses on fire pay an endless visit.
        Chorus   God is like that.
I watched over him like a shepherd over a sheep
While he went bleating and gamboling and flocking around and getting
    fleeced, forgetting whom to worship.
Well, every shepherd knows his way to the butcher shop.
        Chorus   God is in bad shape.
Come, Death. He has made me mad.
I summon Death. For his ingratitude,
Everyman must choke on his daily bread.
        Chorus   God is sick and tired.

Come before His Countenance with a Joyful Leaping

Swiveling flatsoled on the dirt but ready to bound in arches at the nick of
time, spurring yourselves, come all as you are with footbones
rattling like claques, with storking knees careering into the crooked
distance, horning in and out of sight,
Come coasting in circles, rearing, running aground, and flickering up the
air, peeling and flaking away like handbills over the sloping
daylight,
Come lambing and fishing, outflanking the body's heights at a single
stroke, out of breath, out at the elbows, spreading blank palms and
flinching up hillsides hoisted out of mind,
Come at a loss out of manholes and sandtraps, jerking free at the heart,
assaulted and blinking on dislocated ankles, swollen with song from
the twisted wreckage, dying and rigorous after the second wind,
For He is falling apart in His unstrung parbuckles, His beard blown loose
by harmonious unction, His countenance breaking, His fragments
flopping up and around without us to the stretches of morning.

Plainsong for Everyone Who Was Killed Yesterday

You haven't missed anything yet:
One dawn, one breakfast, and a little weather,
The clamor of birds whose names
You didn't know, perhaps some housework,
Homework, or a quick sale.
The trees are still the same color,
And the Mayor is still the mayor, and we're not
Having anything unusual for lunch.
No one has kissed her yet
Or slept with him. Our humdrum lives
Have gone on humming and drumming
Through one more morning.

But for a while, we must consider
What you might have wished
To do or look like. So far,
Thinking of you, no one has forgotten
Anything he wanted to remember.
Your death is fresh as a prize
Vegetable—familiar but amazing,
Admirable but not yet useful—
And you're in a class
By yourself. We don't know
Quite what to make of you.

You've noticed you don't die
All at once. Some people like me
Still offer you our songs
Because we don't know any better
And because you might believe
At last whatever we sing
About you, since no one else is dreaming
Of singing: *Remember that time*
When you were wrong? Well, you were right.
And here's more comfort: all fires burn out
As quickly as they burn. They're over
Before we know it, like accidents.

You may feel you were interrupted
Rudely, cut off in the middle
Of something crucial,
And you may even be right
Today, but tomorrow
No one will think so.
Today consists of millions
Of newsless current events
Like the millions of sticks and stones
From here to the horizon. What are you
Going to miss? The calendar
Is our only program.

Next week or next year
Is soon enough to consider
Those brief occasions you might rather
Not have lost: the strange ones
You might go so far
As to say you could have died for:
Love, for example, or all
The other inflammations of the cerebral
Cortex, the astounding, irreversible
Moments you kept promising yourself
To honor, which are as far away
Now as they always were.

THREE

Muse

Cackling, smelling of camphor, crumbs of pink icing
Clinging to her lips, her lipstick smeared
Halfway around her neck, her cracked teeth bristling
With bloody splinters, she leans over my shoulder.
Oh my only hope, my lost dumbfounding baggage,
My gristle-breasted, slack-jawed zealot, kiss me again.

Words above a Narrow Entrance

The land behind your back
Ends here: never forget
Signpost and weathercock
That turned always to point
Directly at your eyes;
Remember slackening air
At the top of the night,
Your feet treading on space.
The stream, like an embrace,
That swamped you to the throat
Has altered now; the briar
Rattling against your knees,
The warlock in disguise,
The giant at the root—
The country that seemed
Malevolence itself
Has gone back from the heart.

Beyond this gate, there lies
The land of the different mind,
Not honey in the brook,
None of the grass you dreamed.
Foresee water on fire,
And notches in a cloud;
Expect noise from a rock,
And faces falling apart.
The pathway underfoot,
Heaving its dust, will cross
A poisonous expanse
Where light knocks down the trees,
And whatever spells you took
Before, you will take anew
From the clack in the high wind.
Nothing will be at ease,
Nothing at peace, but you.

The Poets Agree to Be Quiet by the Swamp

They hold their hands over their mouths
And stare at the stretch of water.
What can be said has been said before:
Strokes of light like herons' legs in the cattails,
Mud underneath, frogs lying even deeper.
Therefore, the poets may keep quiet.
But the corners of their mouths grin past their hands.
They stick their elbows out into the evening,
Stoop, and begin the ancient croaking.

Advice to the Orchestra

Start like pieces of string:
Lank homeliness attached, maybe, to nothing.
Then oh! my harpies, brush over the rows and thrust
Music like brooms under their chairs, rouse out the cats, the purses, and
    the dust.
Make them all leap up—the ophthalmic trance-breakers, the doggers,
    midge-killers, all the pie-faced gawkies and their crumbs.
Give them music to break their glasses, to knock their eyelids up like
    hatbrims.

When they run, follow them out of doors, out of windows,
Assault their tails with chorts and tootles, oompahs and glissandos.
Snare them. Give them no hiding places. Let them be draked in the reeds.
Slide after them into dumps and suburbs, over trembling hairpin roads,
Across channels and bays to the tilted islands where water whirls on edge.
Spiral through tunnels, over the baffling rocks and the spokes of forests,
    to the last desperate wheelprint, committing outrage.

Oh my outlandish ones,
Offer yourselves through the mold on brass, through skins and bones.
Your music must consume its instruments
Or die lost in the elbow joints and valves, in snaggle and crook, ratchet
    and pinchbeck, in the folded winds.
Let the boom come. Send up the burning brows,
The white domes of your echoes.

Stand in the pit. Strike the sides of your death. Let spherical thunder
Rise from gravel-throated, unharmonious earth, the stricken center,
Beyond air fringed like a curtain, through the cabbage leaves and angels
    of the moon,
The mercurial archangels, rise to untune
The principalities and powers, the squash of the sun, virtues and jovial
    dominations, the saturnine thrones, calliope-pumping cherubim and
    seraphim with their heads ablaze
Against the old gods' mobile, eccentric knees.

That Old Gang of Mine

"Warden, I thank you." "Not at all." He bowed.
With my dress cane, I hit him on the head.

"A stirring evening, Officer." The guard
Blinked at my spinning watch-chain. Then he snored.

"Come out, good thieves," I whispered to the walls,
And heard the fine teeth mousing in the cells.

Sliding the key-ring under the cold bars,
I tiptoed down the hall and out of doors.

The first explosion coughed the windows out;
The second made stones generous to a fault;

The third threw up the prison, clapped its wings,
Squinted the lights, and pierced the sirens' lungs.

Over the rubble in their shredded suits,
Out of the tangle of bent license plates,

Through the dim ruckus between dust and guns,
Came my key men, the unlocked skeletons,

Bumping their knobby knees against the rocks
That once stood tall as hell to shepherd crooks.

"Run for our lives!" I whispered. "First comes grass,
Then shrubs, then trees, then water, and then grace."

Oscar the Bounder ripped his jacket off
And vaulted toward the deep night in the buff.

Phineas the Mouthpiece staggered, his eyes shut,
And hawked to break the thick years in his throat.

Sylvester the One-Man Sack-Race, self-possessed,
Stalked through the brambles, lofty as a post.

Esau the Actor, two feet, four feet, none,
Rose past the willows, flickered, and was gone.

Then out of the heap, the unpacked bloodhounds came
Groggy but eager, snuffling the old game.

Fit to be tied behind them, stumbling guards
Saw their long leashes snarling into braids

As we went crosspath, taking to our heels,
In five directions, tireless through the hills.

At dawn, across the water, over the dunes,
Past the bleak alders and the bleaker downs,

Over the thorn scrub like *cheval-de-frise*,
I went to meet them, purple with their praise,

And as we leaped and crowed in a shower of cash,
We danced a ring around the burning bush.

Every Good Boy Does Fine

I practiced my cornet in a cold garage
Where I could blast it till the oil in drums
Boomed back; tossed free throws till I couldn't move my thumbs;
Sprinted through tires, tackling a headless dummy.

In my first contest, playing a wobbly solo,
I blew up in the coda, alone on stage,
And twisting like my hand-tied necktie, saw the judge
Letting my silence dwindle down his scale.

At my first basketball game, gangling away from home
A hundred miles by bus to a dressing room,
Under the showering voice of the coach, I stood in a towel,
Having forgotten shoes, socks, uniform.

In my first football game, the first play under the lights
I intercepted a pass. For seventy yards, I ran
Through music and squeals, surging, lifting my cleats,
Only to be brought down by the safety man.

I took my second chances with less care, but in dreams
I saw the bald judge slumped in the front row,
The coach and team at the doorway, the safety man
Galloping loud at my heels. They watch me now.

You who have always horned your way through passages,
Sat safe on the bench while some came naked to court,
Slipped out of arms to win in the long run,
Consider this poem a failure, sprawling flat on a page.

Diary

At Monday dawn, I climbed into my skin
And went to see the money. There were the shills:
I conned them—oh, the coins fell out of their mouths,
And paint peeled from the walls like dollar bills.
Below their money-belts, I did them in.

All day Tuesday, grand in my underwear,
I shopped for the world, bought basements and airplanes,
Bargained for corners and pedestrians
And, when I'd marketed the elms away,
Swiped from the water, stole down to the stones.

Suddenly Wednesday offered me my shirt,
Trousers, and shoes. I put them on to dream
Of the one-way stairway and the skittering cloud,
Of the dangerous, footsore crossing at the heart
Where trees, rivers, and stones reach for the dead.

And the next day meant the encircling overcoat
Wherein I sweltered, woolly as a ram:
From butt to swivel, I hoofed it on the loam,
Exacting tribute from the flock in the grass.
My look passed through the werewolf to the lamb.

Friday shied backward, pulling off my clothes:
The overcoat fell open like a throat;
Shirttail and shoe went spidery as a thought,
And covetous drawers whipped knee-deep in a knot.
My skin in a spiral tapered into gold.

And it was naked Saturday for love
Again: the graft grew milky at a kiss.
I lay on the week with money, lust, and vapor,
Megalomania, fear, the tearing-off,
And love in a coil. On Sunday, I wrote this.

The Calculation

A man six feet tall stands on a curb, facing a light suspended fifteen feet
above the middle of a street thirty feet wide. He begins to walk along the curb
at five m.p.h. After he has been walking for ten seconds, at what rate is the
length of his shadow increasing?
   —a problem given by my calculus instructor, Penn State, 1946

Facing a streetlight under batty moths
And June bugs ratcheting like broken clock springs,
I stand, for the sake of a problem, on the curb—
Neither in grass nor gutter—while those wings
Switch down the light and patch my undershirt.

I turn half-right. My shadow cuts a hedge,
Climbs through a rhododendron to a porch,
And nods on a windowsill. How far it goes
I leave to burglars and Pythagoras.
Into the slanting glare I slant my watch,

Then walk five miles per hour, my shoes on edge
In a practiced shuffle past the sewer grid
Over the gold no-parking-or-pausing zones
And into the clear—five seconds—into dirt,
Then over a sawhorse studded with lanterns,

And at the tenth I stiffen like a stump
Whose lopped head ripples with concentric figures,
Note the location of my other head
In a garden, but keep trundling forward,
Ignoring doppelgängers from moon and lawn-lamp,

My eyes alert now, leveling my feet,
Seeing my shadow sweeping like a scythe
Across the stalks of daisies, barking trees,
And scraping up the blistered weatherboard
To the eaves of houses, scaling the rough shingles.

At fifteen seconds, in a vacant lot,
My head lies on a board. I count it off.
I think back to the garden, and I guess,
Instructor, after fifteen years of sweat,
It was increasing five feet plus per second.

At the start, I could have fallen, turned around,
Or crossed to the very center of confusion,
My shadow like a manhole, no one's length,
Or the bulb itself been broken with a shot,
And all my reckoning have gone unreckoned.

But I was late because my shadow was
Pointing toward nothing like the cess of light,
Sir, and bearing your cold hypotenuse—
That cutter of corners, jaywalker of angles—
On top of my head, I walked the rest of the night.

Going to Pieces

Pull yourself together, pal.
    —advice from a stranger

Those marionette show skeletons can do it
Suddenly, after their skulls have been
Alone in the rafters, after their wishbones
Have fluttered in the wings, leaving the feet onstage
To hoof it solo: they pull themselves together,
Bring everything back and thread it on their spines.

But looking around and seeing other people
Coming apart at parties, breaking up
And catching their own laughter in both hands,
Or crossing the lawn and throwing up their spirits
Like voice-balloons in funnies, touching noses
In bedroom mirrors, one after another,
I figure something can be said for it:
Maybe some people break in better halves
Or some of the parts are greater than the whole.

Pal, take a look around: a heap of coats
Discarded in one spot like empty skins;
Under the tables enough shoes and gloves,
Enough loose hair, saliva, and fingernails
To conjure bodies off a hundred souls.
Now I'll tell you one: the palolo worms,
One night a year at the bottom of the sea,
Back halfway out of the burrows where they spend
Long lives; their tails turn luminous, twist free,
And all by themselves swim up to the surface,
Joining with millions of other detached tails;
The sea in a writhing mass lies white for miles
Under a gibbous moon; the bright halves die
And float away like scraps after a party,
But leave behind their larvae, set for life.

Meanwhile, the old ones, steady in their holes
Can go about their business, fanning food
Into their sleek, uninterrupted gullets.
Think of them there, pal, chewing the ocean,
Staying alive by going to pieces.

Making Up for a Soul

It's been like fixing a clock, jamming the wheels,
The pinions, and bent springs into a box
And shaking it. Or like patching a vase,
Gluing the mismatched edges of events
Together despite the quirks in the design.
Or trying to make one out of scraps of paper,
The yellowing, dog-eared pages going slapdash
Over each other, flat as a collage.
I can't keep time with it. It won't hold water.
Ripping and rearranging make no pattern.

Imagine me with a soul: I'm sitting here
In the room with you, smiling from corner to corner,
My chest going up and down with inspiration.
I sit serene, insufferably at my ease,
Not scratching or drumming but merely suffering
Your questions, like the man from the back of the book
With all the answers. You couldn't stand me, could you?

My love, if *you* have a soul, don't tell me yet.
Why can't we simply stay uneasy together?
There are snap-on souls like luminous neckties
That light up in the dark, spelling our names.
Let's put them on for solemn visitors,
Switch off the lights, then grope from room to room,
Making our hollow, diabolical noises
Like Dracula and his spouse, avoiding mirrors,
Clutching each other fiendishly for life
To stop the gaps in ourselves, like better halves.

Walking in the Snow

. . . *if the author had said, "Let us put on appropriate galoshes," there could,*
of course, have been no poem . . .
—*an analysis of Elinor Wylie's "Velvet Shoes,"* College English,
March 1948, p. 319

Let us put on appropriate galoshes, letting them flap open,
And walk in the snow.
The eyes have fallen out of the nearest snowman;
It slumps in its shadow,
And the slush at the curb is gray as the breasts of gulls.
As we slog together
Past arbors and stiff trees, all knocked out cold
At the broken end of winter,
No matter what may be falling out of the sky
Or blowing sideways
Against our hearts, we'll make up our own weather.
Love, stamping our galoshes,
Let's say something inappropriate, something flat
As a scholar's ear
And, since this can't be a poem, something loud
And pointless, leading nowhere
Like our footprints ducking and draking in the snow
One after the other.

On Seeing an X Ray of My Head

Now face to face, hard head, old nodder and shaker,
While we still have ears,
Accept my congratulations: you survived
My headlong blunders
As, night by night, my knuckles beat at your brow
More often than at doors,
Yet you were pampered, waved from the end of your stick
Like a bird in feathers,
Wrapped in towels, whistled and nightcapped,
And pressed into pillows.
I see by this, the outline of our concern,
What you will lose
Before too long: the shadowy half of chin
And prodding nose,
Thatchwork of hair, loose tongue, and parting lips,
My look as blank as yours,
And yet, my madcap, catchall rattlepot,
Nothing but haze
Shows on this picture what we had in mind,
The crannied cauliflower
Ready to boil away at a moment's notice
In a fit of vapors
And leave us holding the bag. Oh my brainpan,
When we start our separate ways
With opaque, immortal fillings clenched in our teeth
Like a bunch of keys,
And when your dome goes rolling into a ditch
And, slack in the jaws,
Stops at a hazard, some unplayable lie,
Accept at your ease
Directly what was yours at one remove:
Light through your eyes,
Air, dust, and water as themselves at last. Keep smiling.
Consider the source.
Go back to the start, old lime pit, remembering flesh and skin,
Your bloody forebears.

The Inexhaustible Hat

The incomparable Monsieur Hartz in 1880
Without assistants, with only three small tables
On a well-lit stage produced from a borrowed hat
Seven glass lanterns, each with a lighted candle,
A swaddle of scarves, hundreds of yards of bunting,
A lady's bustle, a stack of empty boxes,
A cage with a lovely, stuffed, half-cocked canary,
A life-size babydoll and dozens of goblets,
A shower of playing cards, a gentleman's wig,
And lastly a grinning skull. Oh Monsieur Hartz,
You were right, you were absolutely right! Encore!

Waiting on the Curb

Death: "Everyman, stand still."

Stalled by the traffic, waiting for the light
And giving a little at the knees, I stand
As still at others tied up in their shoes.
Looking ahead, my eyes switch out of sight,
Commemorating death by doing nothing
And needing a signal to get over it.

Behind my packages, I sweat it out,
Having already memorized the corner—
The fireplug, street sign, waste-can, cracked cement
With which our city civilizes dirt—
And, feeling cornered, shuffle to keep warm,
Knowing it's useless now to plant my feet.

Ahead of me, all out from under arrest
And rushing suddenly over the jammed street,
The others hurry off to make up time;
But losing this moment, Death, I wait for you
To let me go. My disobedient body
Clings to my spine like a drunk to a lamppost.

House Hunting

The wind has twisted the roof from an old house
      And thrown it away,
And no one's going to live there anymore.
      It tempts me:
Why not have weather falling in every room?
      Isn't the sky
As easy to keep up as any ceiling?
      Less flat and steady?
Rain is no heavier, soaking heavy heads,
      Than a long party.
Imagine moonlight for a chandelier,
      Sun through the laundry,
The snow on conversation, leaves in the bed,
      Fog in the library,
Or yourself in a bathtub hoping for the best
      As the clouds go by,
Dressing for dinner according to what comes down
      And not how many.
And at night, to sit indoors would be to lose
      Nothing but privacy
As the crossing stars took time to mark their flight
      Over the mind's eye.

Lullaby through the Side of the Mouth

Good night, unlucky three. Mice at a feast
Go nibbling the grain away; the wrens
Fluff one another in the hollow post;
And moths are knuckling at the windowpanes.

O pray to the wall, pray to the billypan,
Render all praise to footboards and the sheets,
Call up the spiral mattress if you can:
But see, at your eyes, the counterclockwise lights.

Now you must sacrifice—first, to the dark,
Next, to the crippled underhalf of the mind—
Your faces, hearts, whatever does good work,
Before you come to the burrows at wit's end.

Once more, the holes lie open into dreams:
In one, a hairless tail; in one, a quill;
And, in a third, antennae with soft plumes.
Now put them on, dear Lust, my Love, poor Will.

May forefeet lift each kernel like a cup;
May beak and claw touch heaven under wings;
May the dust-flecked moth find every window up.
But those are joys. You will not dream such things.

The Breaking Point

There are four kinds of stress,
Yet we are not concerned
Today with compression,
Torsion, or simple bending
But (for this unknown substance
No wider than your spine)
Strictly with tension:
You will notice the sample
Is clamped at either end
By a framework designed
To measure the exact strain
Required to break it: this
Experiment might be crucial
To you: if you can learn
Under careful control
At what stress it will fail,
You are forewarned and -armed
Against one small disaster;
Therefore, not knowing
The breaking point
Precisely we begin increasing
Tension, at first seeing
Nothing, but soon on the surface
A change, an ashen look
As the crystal structure goes
Amorphous, and suddenly
The irreversible thinning
Out, the elastic failure,
The crack, the full fracture
At a waist like an hourglass,
The gauge spinning to zero,
And the two jagged halves
Never to be made one
Again except through fire
And the founding hammer.

The First Law of Motion

Staying strictly in line and going
Along with a gag or swinging
Far out and back or simply wheeling
Into the homestretch again and again,
Not shoving or stalling, but coasting
And playing it smooth, pretending
To make light of it, you can seem
To be keeping it up forever, needing
Little or nothing but your own
Dead weight to meet
The demands of momentum,
But there's no way out of touching
Something or being touched, and like it
Or not, you're going to be
Slowing down because turning
A corner means coming to a dead
Halt, however slight, to change direction,
And your impulse to get moving
Again may never move you, so keeping time
Is as inhuman as the strict first law
Of motion, and going off on your own
On some lopsided jagged course
For which there's no equation, some unbecoming
Switchbacked cross-footed trek in a maze
Of your own invention, some dying
Fall no star could fix, is a state of being
Human at least, and so, at last, is stopping.

Song Off-Key

I needed to make music, but look what's coming:
Something offkey, ungainly, with a rat and a bum in it,
A song like a dish of peaches spilled on the floor
With nothing fitting or touching anything else except by flopping
Slice over juice to meet the linoleum.

Who said there should be a song like a split ragbag?
Nobody needs it—a song with a hole in the middle
Through which some garbled, red-wigged, blackfaced gag
Is sticking its head to be conked with baseballs, a song
Like all the wrong weather tangling sunshine and blizzards.

A song should have its tail in its mouth like a hoopsnake,
Or come to a neat point like a stack of belongings,
Or link and labor its opposites in a fixed sword-fight.
Who wants a song like a dump where anything comes or goes?
Here come that rat and that bum for no good reason.

The Trail Horse

If I could get Yeats on a horse, I'd put a new rhythm into English poetry.
—Ezra Pound

Get on, expecting the worst—a mount like a statue
Or a bucking runaway.
If neither happens, if this bay mare holds still,
Then you're off
The ground, not touching the ground except through her
Four stilted corners
Which now plop up and down as carefully
In the mud by the road
As if those hoofprints behind her were permanent.
You're in the saddle
As she clip-clops up the path on a slack rein,
Her nose leading the way
Under the pine boughs switching like her tail.
Give in. Sit still.
It won't be hard to let her have her head:
It's hers by a neck;
She'll keep it against your geeing, hawing, or whoaing.
This one's been bred
To walk from daybreak to darkness in the mountains
Up trail or down
And will do it without you tomorrow. The apparatus
Cinching and bridling her,
The leather and metal restraints for a prisoner
Who *won't* be convenient,
Who *won't* do what she's told or listen to reason,
Are mostly for show:
For example, take this place you're passing now—
Tall stumps and boulders,
Thirty degrees of slope and a narrow trail—
A time for judgment,
A time for the nice control of cause and effect.
Do you see the flies
Clustered around her eyelids, nipping their salt?
Or the humming wasp
Tossed from her tail to her rump where it sinks in?
Suddenly swiveling

And sliding, jerking tight as a slipknot
And rearing out from under
Arched like a cow and a half humped over the moon,
She leaves you alone,
And you part company on the only terms
Possible: hers being yours—
No straddler of winged horses, no budding centaur,
But a man biting the dust.

Song to Accompany the Bearer of Bad News

Kings kill their messengers
Sometimes, slicing wildly
Through pages delivering their grief
And you may do the same
With this page under this poem
Tear it lengthwise first
With feeling, cutting off
Each phrase into meaningless halves
Then crossways, severing
The mild beginning from the bad ending
By now you know the worst
Having imagined the remainder
Down to the painful inch
Where something like your name
Closes this message
You needn't finish now
You may stop here
And puzzle it out later.

Kings kill
Sometimes, slicing
Through pages
And you may
With this page
Tear it
With feeling
Each phrase
Then crossways
The mild beginning
By now you know
Having imagined
Down to
Where something
Closes
You needn't finish
You may stop
And puzzle it out.

Their messengers
Wildly
Delivering their grief
Do the same
Under this poem
Lengthwise first
Cutting off
Into meaningless halves
Severing
The bad ending
The worst
The remainder
The painful inch
Like your name
This message
Now
Here
Later

You may   tear it   into meaningless halves
Lengthwise first   then crossways
Severing   something like   the painful inch
Later   under this poem   messengers
Delivering their grief   puzzle it out
Having imagined   the worst
Kings kill   wildly   through pages
Cutting off   the bad ending
Do the same   with this page
By now you know   the mild beginning
Down to where   your name   closes
With feeling   now   you may stop.

From *Who Shall Be the Sun?* **(1978)**

Searching in the Britannia Tavern

To Earl Lund, Clallam tribe

To get to the Land of the Dead, you must go through
The place where everything is flying, past falling water
To the curb, across the sidewalk, stumbling, to the hunting ground.
Sleeping by day and moving only by night, you will come
To the place where you must sink, then rise, then enter
The abrupt silence where they have hidden your soul.

Having no one to be, the Dead steal souls. They lie
In wait in the middle of the floor, or spraddle for balance,
Their eyes burnt out. Those climbing toward the door
Have never entered. Those descending never arrive. They stand
Facing in different directions, blinking at walls, remembering
Nothing about your life. Remember, you told me:

Only a spirit can grapple with the Dead.
It must be danced or it never appears. You must watch for it
At night, or walk all day in your sleep, or stay underwater
To make it come to you. When it enters, nothing stands still.
The wall is the floor, the floor and ceiling are walls,
Its voice is breaking in your ears, its broken speech
Is saying what you must know, the Dead are falling
Against each other, rattling their helpless fingers, remember,
The First People changed into bears, into rocks and fish,
Into trees, beavers, and birds, when they learned that men were coming,
And there, stalking toward you, the dark one is Tah-mah-no-us,
One Who Has Never Changed, his terrible mouth is smiling, he bears
Your soul slowly toward you in cupped hands.

Old Man, Old Man

Young men, not knowing what to remember,
Come to this hiding place of the moons and years,
To this Old Man. Old Man, they say, where should we go?
Where did you find what you remember? Was it perched in a tree?
Did it hover deep in the white water? Was it covered over
With dead stalks in the grass? Will we taste it
If our mouths have long lain empty?
Will we feel it between our eyes if we face the wind
All night, and turn the color of earth?
If we lie down in the rain, can we remember sunlight?

He answers, I have become the best and worst I dreamed.
When I move my feet, the ground moves under them.
When I lie down, I fit the earth too well.
Stones long underwater will burst in the fire, but stones
Long in the sun and under the dry night
Will ring when you strike them. Or break in two.
There were always many places to beg for answers:
Now the places themselves have come in close to be told.
I have called even my voice in close to whisper with it:
Every secret is as near as your fingers.
If your heart stutters with pain and hope,
Bend forward over it like a man at a small campfire.

Fog

Though your brothers, after the long hunt and the fasting,
After holding still, have found Fox, Bear Mother,
Or Snake at their sides and taken them
Into the empty mouths of their spirits,
Do not be jealous. They will be cunning
Or strong or good at dreaming. Do not be ashamed
That you—when the day changed, when the first hour
Came falling suddenly over the last hour—
Found only Fog as the eye of your heart opened.

Now when your feet touch earth, nothing will know you.
You will move without moving a leaf,
Climb the steep cliffside as easily as Hawk,
Cross water, pass silently as Owl.
You will become trees by holding them inside you,
And tall stones, become a whole valley
Where birds fall still, where men stay close to fires.
You without wings or hands will gleam against them,
They will breathe you, they will be lost in you,
Your song will be the silence between their songs,
Your white darkness will teach them,
You will wrap all love and fear in a beautiful blindness.

Salmon Boy

That boy was hungry. His mother gave him Dog Salmon,
Only the head. It was not enough,
And he carried it hungry to the river's mouth
And fell down hungry. Saltwater came from his eyes,
And he turned over and over. He turned into it.

And that boy was swimming under the water
With his round eyes open. He could not close them.
He was breathing the river through his mouth.
The river's mouth was in *his* mouth. He saw stones
Shimmering under him. Now he was Salmon Boy.

He saw the Salmon People waiting. They said, "This water
Is our wind. We are tired of swimming against the wind.
Come to the deep, calm valley of the sea.
We are hungry too. We must find the Herring People."
And they turned their green tails. Salmon Boy followed.

He saw Shell-Walking-Backward, Woman-Who-Is-Half-Stone.
He heard the long, high howling of Wolf Whale,
Seal Woman's laughter, the whistling of Sea Snake,
Saw Loon Mother flying through branches of seaweed,
Felt Changer turn over far down in his sleep.

He followed to the edge of the sky where it opens
And closes, where Moon opens and closes forever,
And the Herring People brought feasts of eggs,
As many as stars, and Salmon Boy ate the stars
As if he flew among them, saying *Hungry, Hungry.*

But the Post of Heaven shook, and the rain fell
Like pieces of Moon, and the Salmon People swam,
Tasting sweet, saltless wind under the water,
Opening their mouths again to the river's mouth,
And Salmon Boy followed, full-bellied, not afraid.

He swam fastest of all. He leaped into the air
And smacked his blue-green silvery side, crying, *Eyo!*
I jump! again and again. Oh, he was Salmon Boy!
He could breathe everything! He could see everything!
He could eat everything! And then his father speared him.

He lay on the riverbank with his eyes open,
Saying nothing while his father emptied his belly.
He said nothing when his mother opened him wide
To dry in the sun. He was full of the sun.
All day he dried on sticks, staring upriver.

Who Shall Be the Sun?

The People said, "Who shall be the sun?"
Raven cried, "Raven! Raven!"
He imagined rising and setting
Grandly, his great wings spreading over the People.
All days would belong to him. No one
Would see the earth without marvelous Raven.

He rose then out of the thick night.
He crooked his ragged wings, flapping them wildly,
Yet he made evening all day long,
Nothing but gloom in the woods, shade on the rivers.
The People grunted: "Get away from the sky!
You are too dark! Come down, foolish Raven!"

The People said, "Someone else must try."
Hawk screamed, "Hawk! Hawk!"
He imagined rising and rising
High over the specks of the tiny People.
He would be alone, taller than the wind. No one
Would cast a shadow without brilliant Hawk.

He rose then out of the empty night.
He soared and climbed into the yellow air
As high as noon, clenching his talons,
His bright wings flashing in the eye of the heavens.
The People squinted and shouted: "Too much daylight!
Get out of the sky! Come down, ignorant Hawk!"

The People said, "But we must have someone."
Coyote howled, "Coyote! Coyote!"
He imagined jumping and running
Low over the bent heads of the People.
He would make them crouch all day. No one
Would escape the tricks of clever Coyote.

He rose then out of the hole of night.
He darted and leaped over the red clouds
As swift as stormfire, his jaws gleaming,
His wild breath burning over the crowns of trees.
The People sweated and sputtered, diving into water,
"You will cook the earth! Come down, crazy Coyote!"

The People said, "We shall have no sun at all!"
But Snake whispered, "I have dreamed I was the sun."
Raven, Hawk, and Coyote mocked him by torchlight:
"You cannot scream or howl! You cannot run or fly!
You cannot burn, dazzle, or blacken the earth!
How can you be the sun!" "By dreaming," Snake whispered.

He rose then out of the rich night.
He coiled in a ball, low in the sky.
Slowly he shed the Red Skin of Dawn,
The Skin of the Blue Noontime, the Skin of Gold,
And last the Skin of Darkness, and the People
Slept in their lodges, safe, till he coiled again.

How Coyote Became Rock's Brother

Coyote walked far, lost in the heat of the day.
Sweating, he sat on Rock and said, "My brother,
You may have my robe." He threw it aside
Over Rock's heavy shoulders and wandered on.

A great cloud blackened the earth. Coyote turned
And hurried back to Rock sitting still and dry.
Coyote said, "Give me my robe against the rain."
Rock whispered through the robe, "Now it is mine."

"You have no need of a robe," Coyote said and snatched it
And wrapped it around him, walking into the storm.
But soon, behind, he heard something like thunder
And saw Rock rumbling after him: "Give me my robe!"

Coyote ran past Nighthawk, crying, "Help me! Help me!
Rock is chasing us all!" But Nighthawk said, "No.
Rock is my nest. All night I ride on the wind,
All day I sleep on Rock: he is my day-cloud."

Coyote ran past Buffalo, crying, "Save me! Save me!
Rock wants to kill us all!" But Buffalo
Said, "No. When the People hunt me, Rock deceives them:
We look the same. He splits their strongest arrows."

Coyote ran past Bear, crying, "Only you can help me!
Rock wants to crush us all!" But Bear said, "No.
Rock is the roof of my lodge. He lasts through the Moon
Of the Cracking Trees. He is my winter sky."

Coyote stood alone in the rain then, and Rock tumbled
Closer and closer, bumping and booming.
He was no day-cloud. He was no good protector
Against the shafts of the hunting weather.

Kneeling, Coyote offered his robe again, and Rock
Halted against his forehead, solid and cold.
"I need no robe," Rock said. "I wear this rain.
Tomorrow I wear the sun or the snow, no matter."

Coyote opened his arms and clung to Rock. Rock said,
"I hear your heart. Now you may stand against me.
No one will hunt you. You may sleep beneath me
With or without a robe. Welcome, lost brother."

How Stump Stood in the Water

Ice had many sons. "Find me my food!" he shouted.
They searched in the air and under the water
And brought him Quail and Mussel, Goose and Oyster,
Blue Teal and Rock Crab, Widgeon and Salmon.

"More! More!" Ice shouted. "My sons must feed me!"
Some climbed after Eagle and fell. Some paddled
After Gray Whale and drowned. Some offered
Buzzard and Minnow, Coot and Sea Slug.

But Stump stood in the ocean, catching nothing.
"Foolish Stump! " Ice shouted. "What are you standing on?
What are you holding in your shut hands?
Feed me! Feed me!" But Stump said, "Father,

What am I standing on? What am I holding?
If you tell me, they will be yours forever."
Ice shouted, "You are standing on Flounder!
You have stolen the last sweet eggs of Killdeer

For your selfish dinner! The tide is rising!
Who brings me nothing will come to nothing!"
Then Ice pulled back his other sons to the north,
And the water rose, and the water ebbed away,

And on the barren shore, Stump stood alone
On his own feet, holding his life in his hands.

How Raven Stole Light

The People lived in darkness without Stars,
Unable to hunt or fish, as quiet as ghosts,
But Raven knew where Sun and Moon were hidden.
He flew through a sky as dark as his own feathers
And found a lodge surrounded by daylight.

A great chief lived there with his only daughter.
She came to their water hole, and Raven changed
Into a hemlock needle floating across it.
She drank him, and he grew and grew inside her
Till she lay down on moss and Raven was born.

That chief doted on Raven: his black eyes gleamed,
His beak and tongue were quick, he would play with furs
And bundles of dried light. But Raven saw,
High at the ceiling, three shut bentwood boxes
And knew what they held. He began crying and crying.

They gave him deer-hoof rattles and crowberries,
But still he cried and pointed at those boxes.
They gave him shells and the sweet backbones of salmon,
But he cried and pointed, so the chief brought down
The Box of Stars and gave it to Raven.

He opened it, and there, like herring eggs,
The Stars glistened in clusters, and Raven laughed,
Tossing them through the smoke hole where they tumbled
Across the sky forever. The chief was angry
And closed that smoke hole, scolding at Raven.

So Raven cried for days and would eat nothing,
Would play with nothing, pointing at those boxes.
His eyes turned many colors. He squealed. His mother
Feared he would choke and die, so the chief took down
The second box and gave it to Raven.

He opened it, and Moon gleamed like a fire,
Like pitch-wood burning, like burning candlefish.
He rolled that Moon around the floor of the lodge,
Singing and laughing, but then he cried again
And pointed to the last box on the ceiling.

Closing his ears, the chief brought down that box,
And Raven took it, seizing Moon in his beak,
Broke through the smoke hole, rolled Moon in the sky,
Opened the Box of Sun for the ghostly People,
And flew among them, scattering daylight.

Song for the Bones of Salmon

I have counted your bones,
Salmon, my sister,
Even the thin gillbones
Like the nets of Spider.
Only a few are broken.
Let this song be those bones.

Let it be the scales lost
On the hard stones
Where you strained at nesting.
Let my song be your cupped eye
Where the flies have come for days
As if to the last spring.

Let it be your flesh,
The long muscles stronger
Than the white water.
Let my song fill your mouth
Like your own strange breath,
The wind inside the river.

Now go downstream swiftly,
Your mouth to its mouth.
Take my song into the salt.
Feed long, feed for us both,
And I will wait gladly
Till you come again to die.

Song for the Coming of Smallpox

At night sparks fly from them,
The ships of the Iron People.
Iron struck in the fire
Throws sparks, makes knives
And spearpoints harder than bone.

Wherever those sparks fall
They burn our smooth faces.
They burn, making holes
As deep as bone,
Setting fire to our bodies.

My spirit, when it first came,
Made a hole in my mind,
And I fell down, dreaming
What I must do and be
Through the long fire of my life.

The hole of my mouth
And the hole of my lost eye
Filled with new songs,
But the ships of the Iron People
Bring the mask of many holes.

Who wears it must fall down
With many holes in his mind,
Not iron in that fire,
Not stronger and harder,
But dreaming only of bones.

Song of a Man Who Rushed at the Enemy

I could have fought like Fox who can see behind him,
Who can bite even while running away, or like Owl
Who will hide deep in his hollow but will not surrender.

I could have fought like Snake who only waits to be told
Belong to this place where you are sleeping to stay quiet
But who strikes what comes toward him till he is broken.

But I must rush at my enemy like Bear Mother and Badger
Who know already how to sleep under the ground, or Wolverine
Who will not turn away, who will fight even with Earthmaker.

Now I am running on the shore toward the Iron People,
Toward their smoke and firesticks, against their spitting stones.
I am running faster than Dragonfly who needs to sing nothing.

I am running toward them on the shore forever, singing this.

Death Song

I touch the earth on all fours like a child,
And now my forehead touches the earth.
For the sake of my joys, Sleepmaker, let me in.
I have turned away from none of the six directions.
I have praised the rising and the dying wind,
Water falling or vanishing, even the end of grass.
I have welcomed the seasons equally
And been one with all weather from the wild to the silent.
The only blood left on my hands is my own: now my heart
Will be strict, admitting none, letting none go.
Close all my mouths. I will sleep inside of sleep,
Honoring the gift of darkness till it breaks.
I sing for a cold beginning.

Burial Song

My body ran on its legs and waved its hands,
Dug holes, cracked wood. It leaped into water,
Leaped out again, made fire, flinched from fire.
It climbed over rocks and hurried from one place to another
And came back to its beginning, aiming its empty ears
And eyes into the four mouths of the wind.
My body carried another body into the woods,
Forgot itself, found itself, lost itself.

Now it lies still. Children may tease it with sticks
Or women call to it, laughing behind their fingers,
Or men challenge it with their proud crowing,
But it wants nothing from them and will not move.
Its hands stay where they belong—together—
Its eyes shut, its heels not rising or dragging,
And its mouth keeping a cold council.

My body has stopped. Now yours will go forward,
But mine will stay in this Now, exactly here.
Tomorrow it will seem far behind you.
Though you squint till you weep, you will not see it
Nor will Hawk from the edge of his cloud
Nor will Owl see it in this different darkness.
Yet it will lie in wait for you to remember
Like a dream stiffened with danger.

From *Through the Forest: New and Selected Poems, 1977–87*

ONE

After the Speech to the Librarians

I was speaking to the Librarians,
And now I'm standing at the end of a road,
Having taken a wrong turn going home.
I don't remember what I said.
Something about reading and writing
And not enough about listening and singing.
The gate to this dude ranch is locked,
And a dozen riderless horses are browsing
On the hillside in the gold grass.
On a post, a marsh hawk is holding still,
One eye on me and one on the field
Where hundreds of sparrow-sized water pipits
Are darting and whistling to themselves.
Not even thinking of opening a thesaurus,
I say on behalf of the Librarians, *Beautiful.*

Beyond barbed wire, a cracked water tank
And a wrecked shed: you could wait there
A long time for a school bus.
Whoever locked the gate meant No Thank You,
Not Today, but it wasn't much use.
Everything is trespassing as easily
As the hazy sunlight and these burnt-gold-breasted birds
Taking their sweet time under the hawk's eye,
Even perching beside him, extremely happy
To be where they are and what they are,
And the horses with nothing on their backs
Have opened their own gates for the winter,
And the Librarians are going back to their books
In hundreds and hundreds of schools where children
Will be reading and writing and keeping quiet
Maybe and listening to how not to be so childish.

When I wasn't looking, the hawk flew suddenly,
Skimming the field, effortlessly graceful, tilting
And scanning at low level: he stops
Dead without slowing down, swivels
And drops into the grass, flashing white
And tawny, rises at full speed carrying nothing
And goes on soaring, slanting downhill
No higher than my head, making his sharp outcry.
The water pipits answer, thin as fence wire.
Isn't it wonderful not being dead yet?
Their breasts all hold the same air
As his and the softly whickering unsaddled horses'
And mine and the Librarians'
With which we all might sing for the children.

Sharp-Shin

He broke past the corners
Of our eyes before we could see, before
We could quite catch
Sight of him already beyond
The fence and the next yard and back
Again in full flight, the sharp-shinned
Hawk, an amber and slate streak
Through the morning air after
A blur of a pine siskin, zigzagging
But (like our eyes) not quite touching it, not quite
Taking it in a swirling S-curve
Through vine maple up in a flare
Of tail stripes and dark coverts
To a hemlock branch to perch
Dead still, his claws empty.

Still breathing, we waited. The towhees,
The song sparrows, the juncos
Huddled in thickets, and the quick yellow-
And-gray-streaked siskins flocked
Quivering in a fir tree,
Waiting. The whole broad yard
Fell silent, and nothing moved
Anywhere, not even the one cloud.

He waited too, his breast the shade
Of dead leaves, his blue-gray wings
Folded like bark. The dimmed fire coals
Of his eyes held all of us
There, slow minute
After minute, where we were.

Finally, gradually, one siskin forgot
Where it was, where it had been and why
It had ever been afraid, remembered
Simply wanting to be
Somewhere else that moment and flew
At last from there only
To there in the open, and instantly
So swiftly nothing could know
Exactly when he began the sharp-shin
Burst out of cover around
And up in a tight swerve, struck
Without a pause, and was gone
Deep through the green tree-crown
That made no stir or murmur,
And all fell still once more
While out of his sharp talons
The sharper hook of his beak
Took its share of spring.

Return to the Swamp

To begin again, I come back to the swamp,
To its rich decay, its calm disorder,
To alders with their reddening catkins, to hummocks
Of marsh grass floating on their own living and dead
Abundance, and wait on the shore. From my shallow angle,
Even shallows turn solid: a cast-off sky,
A rough sketching of clouds, a bearable version
Of the sun in a mist, the upside down redoubling
Of cattails, and my eyes, shiftless,
Depending on surface tension like water striders.

What did I hope to find? This crystal gazing
Brings me no nearer what the mergansers know
Or the canvasbacks keeping their distance or the snipes
Whirring away from me, cackling, their beaks downturned,
Heads cocked for my false alarm as they swivel
Loudly and jaggedly into the next bog.
Here among shotgun shells and trampled blackberries,
How can I shape, again, something from nothing?

Edgy and mute, I wait at the edge,
And a bass taking a fly—a splashing master,
Ringmaster of refracted light—remakes the world,
Rippling out beautiful exchanges of stress
And yield, upheaval and rearrangement, scattering
And then regathering the shards of the day,
And suddenly near, there, near in the water
Where he's been floating motionless all this hour,
The hump-browed bullfrog staring at me close-mouthed,
Fixing on me his green, princely attention.

The Author of *American Ornithology* Sketches a Bird, Now Extinct

Alexander Wilson, Wilmington, N.C., 1809

When he walked through town, the wing-shot bird he'd hidden
Inside his coat began to cry like a baby,
High and plaintive and loud as the calls he'd heard
While hunting it in the woods, and goodwives stared
And scurried indoors to guard their own from harm.

And the innkeeper and the goodmen in the tavern
Asked him whether his child was sick, then laughed,
Slapped knees, and laughed as he unswaddled his prize,
His pride and burden: an ivory-billed woodpecker
As big as a crow, still wailing and squealing.

Upstairs, when he let it go in his workroom,
It fell silent at last. He told at dinner
How devoted masters of birds drawn from the life
Must gather their flocks around them with a rifle
And make them live forever inside books.

Later, he found his bedspread covered with plaster
And the bird clinging beside a hole in the wall
Clear through to already splintered weatherboards
And the sky beyond. While he tied one of its legs
To a table leg, it started wailing again

And went on wailing as if toward cypress groves
While the artist drew and tinted on fine vellum
Its red cockade, gray claws, and sepia eyes
From which a white wedge flowed to the lame wing
Like light flying and ended there in blackness.

He drew and studied for days, eating and dreaming
Fitfully through the dancing and loud drumming
Of an ivory bill that refused pecans and beetles,
Chestnuts and sweet-sour fruit of magnolias,
Riddling his table, slashing his fingers, wailing.

He watched it die, he said, with great regret.

Thoreau and the Snapping Turtle

*[It] looked not merely repulsive, but to some extent terrible even as a
crocodile . . . a very ugly and spiteful face.*
    —Thoreau, Journal, *May 17, 1854*

As his boat glided across a flooded meadow,
He saw beneath him under lily pads,
Brown as dead leaves in mud, a yard-long
Snapping turtle staring up through the water
At him, its shell as jagged as old bark.

He plunged his arm in after it to the shoulder,
Stretching and missing, but groping till he caught it
By the last ridge of its tail. Then he held on,
Hauled it over the gunwale, and flopped it writhing
Into the boat. It began gasping for air

Through a huge gray mouth, then suddenly
Heaved its hunchback upward, slammed the thwart
As quick as a spring trap and, thrusting its neck
Forward a foot at a lunge, snapped its beaked jaws
So violently, he only petted it once,

Then flinched away. And all the way to the landing
It hissed and struck, thumping the seat
Under him hard and loud as a stake-driver.
It was so heavy, he had to drag it home,
All thirty pounds of it, wrong side up by the tail.

His neighbors agreed it walked like an elephant,
Tilting this way and that, its head held high,
A scarf of ragged skin at its throat. It would sag
Slowly to rest then, out of its element,
Unable to bear its weight in this new world.

Each time he turned it over, it tried to recover
By catching at the floor with its claws, by straining
The arch of its neck, by springing convulsively,
Tail coiling snakelike. But finally it slumped
On its spiky back like an exhausted dragon.

He said he'd seen a cutoff snapper's head
That would still bite at anything held near it
As if the whole of its life were mechanical,
That a heart cut out of one had gone on beating
By itself like clockwork till the following morning.

And the next week he wrote: *It is worth the while*
To ask ourselves . . . Is our life innocent
Enough? Do we live inhumanely, *toward man*
Or beast, in thought or act? To be successful
And serene we must be at one with the universe.

The least conscious and needless injury
Inflicted on any creature is
To its extent a suicide. What peace—
Or life—can a murderer have? . . . White maple keys
Have begun to fall and float downstream like wings.

There are myriads of shad-flies fluttering
Over the dark still water under the hill.

148

Bears

Out of shadows as deep as shadows
In the woods, the bears come swaying
On their hind legs, the black pads
Of forepaws reaching forward, their foreheads
Higher than all the men now running
Behind them into the charmed circle,
Into the ring and the glaring spotlight,
Now pausing, lifting their muzzles, turning
To a blare of horns, they begin dancing
At the ends of leashes, their fur gleaming
All shades of fallen leaves by moonlight,
Up on red globes and walking, not falling
Off, they waddle steadily, swiftly
To the feet of silver trees and climb them
To other trees, descending, they swivel
Firesticks in their claws, they ride
On wheels so surely, so heavily
They seem to spiral downward without
Stopping, and now they are swaying away
On sawdust to drumbeats, to applause
Like heartbeats while men are running behind them
Becoming shadows again among shadows.

Games

The children from the nursery school are running
Slowly, zigzaggedly on the grass at the zoo,
Trying to catch the chickens that run free
Among the bushes and always get away.

The game is called Chasing Something. You play it
Squawking and clucking, wonderfully unhappy
Not to be able to touch those feathers ruffling
And flapping, squawking back at you out of fear.

You wear your name and the name of your keeper
And don't pay any attention to each other
Or to lions or llamas or boas or kangaroos.
You want your game to be right out in the open

Where you can reach for it with friendly fingers
And crow out loud to say how eager you are,
How hungry to learn a game called Catching Something.
But if you catch it, then what do you do?

Do you start a zoo and fill it with wild playthings
Waiting behind bars to look at children
Chasing more chickens under the maple trees?
You don't catch anything yet. Keepers catch *you.*

They make you sit together and play Yelling
And Eating and Drinking and Dropping Sandwiches.
The chickens gather around you quietly
And play their game called Come to the Picnic.

Photographing a Rattlesnake

On smooth sand among stones
It stares more steadily
And lidlessly than the lens
Held near it, not hiding
Or posing, but simply there
In a dead calm, dead sure
Of the ways of its body
Around the maze past the end
Of nerves to the inmost
Rattle, but suddenly
The wedge of the blunt
Straightforward head, S-curve
Of muscle straight
Forward in a blur, mouth wide
For a down-slanted stabbing
Of fangs, a thump
At the camera's glassy eye,
Then a slow turning-away
Out of spirals from the sun
To shadows, to be scattered
Out of plain sight
Into mica spilled on pebbles
Over diamonds seen through
A teardrop of venom
Back to its still life.

Washing a Young Rhinoceros

Inside its horse-high, bull-strong, hog-tight fence
It will stand beside you in a concrete garden,
Leaning your way
All thousand pounds of its half-grown body
To meet the water pouring out of your hose
The temperature of September.

And as slowly its patina (a gray compounded
Of peanut shells and marshmallows, straw and mud)
Begins to vanish
From the solid rib cage and the underbelly
Under your scrub brush, you see, wrinkled and creased
As if in thought, its skin

From long upper lip to fly-whisk gleam in the sun,
Erect ears turning backward to learn how
You hum your pleasure,
And eyelashes above the jawbone hinges
Fluttering wetly as it waits transfixed
(The folds at the four leg-pits

Glistening pink now) for you never to finish
What feels more wonderful than opening
And closing its empty mouth
Around lettuce and grapes and fresh bouquets of carrots
And cabbage leaves, what feels as good to desire
As its fabulous horn.

Sitting by a Swamp

Minutes ago, it was dead:
This swamp when I first came
Fell still as if poisoned,
The air expiring, cattails
Bent and brought to nothing
By the motionless water.

Now first the sunfish rising
To touch the underface
Of the pool, a muttered frog-call,
And out of the willow roots
From crushed stems and stubble
The *chap* of a marsh wren,

From a thicket a fox sparrow
Taking me in, one eye
At a wary time, where I wait
To be what they want me to be:
Less human. A dragonfly
Burns green at my elbow.

Loons Mating

Their necks and their dark heads lifted into a dawn
Blurred smooth by mist, the loons
Beside each other are swimming slowly
In charmed circles, their bodies stretched underwater
Through ripples quivering and sweeping apart
The gray sky now held close by the lake's mercurial threshold
Whose face and underface they share
In wheeling and diving tandem, rising together
To swell their breasts like swans, to go breasting forward
With beaks turned down and in, near shore,
Out of sight behind a windbreak of birch and alder,
And now the haunted uprisen wailing call,
And again, and now the beautiful sane laughter.

Whisper Song

Listening and listening
Closely, you may hear
(After its other
Incredibly clear song)
The one the winter wren
Sings in the thinnest of whispers
More quietly than soft rain
Proclaiming almost nothing
To itself and to you,
And you must be
Only a step away
To hear it even faintly
(No one knows why
It will sing so softly),
Its tiny claws
Braced for arpeggios,
Its dark eyes
Gleaming with a small
Astonishing promise,
Its beak held open
For its hushed throat,
Whispering to itself
From its mysterious heart.

Kingfisher

The blunt big slate-blue dashing cockaded head
Cocked and the tapering thick of the bill
Sidelong for a black eye staring down
From the elm branch over the pool now poised
Exactly for this immediate moment diving
In a single wingflap wingfold plunging
Slapwash not quite all the way under
The swirling water and upward instantly
In a swerving spiral back to the good branch
With a fingerling catfish before the ripples
Have reached me sitting nearby to follow it
With a flip of a shake from crestfeathers to white
Bibchoker down the crawhatch suddenly
Seeing me and swooping away cackling
From the belt streaked rusty over the full belly.

Chorus

That rain-strewn night in the woods, the *chorus, chorus*
Of the green tree frogs called us
And led us by flashlight far from our firelight
Over and down a logging road to the marsh,

And they kept singing as green as the half-frozen
Hemlock branches we brushed slowly among,
As high and thin as the air we tried to hold
As breath among mountains, as thin

And clear as the ice our boots were breaking
Gently, each step a pale-green croaking
Of its own, as we came nearer and nearer where
They had risen out of cold graves to the cold

At the brittle edge of winter broken toward spring
To make their music over a cold spawning,
To choir all night after night, telling each other
We lived at the end of summer, we live

Here again and again. As we came closer,
The singing ended, suddenly went silent
At a single pulsing throatbeat. Nothing but wind
And sleet made any sound over the marsh.

We turned our light away. We waited longer
And longer in darkness, shivering like the reeds
Beyond us, chilled as the film of ice at our feet,
Forgetting all words, and the first voice began

Again, far off, and slowly the green others
Nearby began their hesitant answers, their answers
Louder and clearer chorused around us
As if we belonged there, as if we belonged to them.

The Source

Neither had said they were going to climb to it,
But they kept walking beside the stream
Under the high shade
Of fir trees, upslope, wading through ferns and leaves
As if through a living and dying current,
Through water itself
Whenever the sea-green walls of the creek bank
Steepened to overhangs where roots
Clung wrong-side up
And seedling firs lurched out from under a world
That dared them to survive one birth.
They shared smooth stones
With sandpipers and dippers, with gold-eyed frogs,
Shared low-slung branches with green herons,
With kingfishers,
Warblers, and winter wrens, who watched them pass
Songless to higher ground, to a light
Thinning out, a waterfall
Where the creek was rain and a sideways mist and past
The sidelong mouths of tunnels and freshets
Glistening, as cold
To their fingers' touch as the promises of winter.
More shallow, its stones no longer softened
By white-water crowfoot and pale
Flowerless fountain moss, the creek seemed younger,
Hurrying, its surface quick, more hectic,
As if it felt no longing
Yet to have anything like the sea to turn to.
They climbed past thicker and smaller trees,
Past the half-dead
And the weathered barkless gray dead at the treeline,
Climbed toward spillways of snow on the mountain
Through avalanche lily, sorrel,
Through lupine, through snow, the light a snowfall,
A blue-white daylight the color of snow-melt
Shimmering by their feet,

Still only half persuaded not to be ice
But to give in to the full beginning
Of flowing. At the rim
Of a pond near the foot of steep snow-drifted talus,
Half-frozen, they knelt where the foot-wide creek
Was now being born
Again and again under their eyes. They drank
From the source, their blue lips going numb
At that strange kiss.
They kissed like strangers. They watched the creek spill over
Stones like first words: *Only
Begin, and the rest will follow.*

Getting There

You take a final step and, look, suddenly
You're there. You've arrived
At the one place all your drudgery was aimed for:
This common ground
Where you stretch out, pressing your cheek to sandstone.
What did you want
To be? You'll remember soon. You feel like tinder
Under a burning glass,
A luminous point of change. The sky is pulsing
Against the cracked horizon,
Holding it firm till the arrival of stars
In time with your heartbeats.
Like wind etching rock, you've made a lasting impression
On the self you were
By having come all this way through all this welter
Under your own power,
Though your traces on a map would make an unpromising
Meandering lifeline.
What have you learned so far? You'll find out later,
Telling it haltingly
Like a dream, that lost traveler's dream
Under the last hill
Where through the night you'll take your time out of mind
To unburden yourself
Of elements along elementary paths
By the break of morning.
You've earned this worn-down, hard, incredible sight
Called Here and Now.
Now, what you make of it means everything,
Means starting over:
The life in your hands is neither here nor there
But getting there,
So you're standing again and breathing, beginning another
Journey without regret
Forever, being your own unpeaceable kingdom,
The end of endings.

TWO

Feeding

When I dropped bread, they swam
Out of nowhere, the fingerling
Catfish, even darker
Than the pool lying dead calm
Over them and around them.

Those inches of black ribbon
All held white crumbs like eyes
And wavered themselves away
In schools and disappeared
Again into deeper water.

When I dropped more, what came
Was an altogether stranger
Nature of moving slow,
As though the elders knew
They could be slow to swim

But would still be in time
To take what was their own
Into their own gloom
Of soft-barbed opening
And closing jaws and turn

Away in easy curves
With a sinewy suppleness,
Undulant, fading down
To what they might become
Somewhere still more dim.

When I broke the final crust,
What rose to the underface
Of the pond (so slow, it seemed
Too slow to lift a form
That huge from so far under)

Has kept its place in the night
Of my mind since I was four,
Moving its perfectly sure,
Unhurried, widening mouth
Toward whiteness to darken it.

Boy Jesus

When they made me the boy Jesus
In the Sunday school Christmas pageant, oh Jesus,
I would have given almost anything
To be anybody else in the world but a made-up Jesus.

But suddenly it was too late to say anything
Polite against it or do anything
Desperate in my knee-length toga, while my squirming friends
Snickered in the pews, or even *feel* anything

As I floated down the endless aisle, praying those friends
Would forget someday and be real friends
And not remember me forever singing that damned song
In a shaky soprano, "All Men Be Loving Friends."

It would have been terrible enough singing any song
In public, even the school fight song,
But to have to look so holy-faced and fluttery while I,
Of all young sinners, sang it, made it my swan song.

Why had they picked on me? Jesus and I
Gave each other a pain: I couldn't stump preachers, could I?
No dove had come flapping down when I was baptized, I was no boy
Genius, and we were Laurel and Hardy carpenters, my father and I.

And my voice was breaking: I was only half a boy,
A sneak thief, liar, prober of loveless keyholes, a would-be boy
Magician, a card-stacker more ruled by swear-words
Than by Jesus Christ Almighty, the Good Boy.

From that day on, I put my fidgety faith in my own words
And later in love—in ugly, profane, beautiful words,
Instead of going hook, line, and sinker for Jesus—
No Gospels for the Fishers of Men, but love in other words.

The Junior High School Band Concert

When our semi-conductor
Raised his baton, we sat there
Gaping at *Marche Militaire*,
Our mouth-opening number.
It seemed faintly familiar
(We'd rehearsed it all that winter),
But we attacked in such a blur,
No army anywhere
On its stomach or all fours
Could have squeezed through our cross fire.

I played cornet, seventh chair
Out of seven, my embouchure
A glorified Bronx cheer
Through that three-keyed keyhole stopper
And neighborhood window slammer
Where mildew fought for air
At every exhausted corner,
My fingering still unsure
After scaling it for a year
Except on the spit-valve lever.

Each straight-faced mother and father
Retested his moral fiber
Against our traps and slurs
And the inadvertent whickers
Paradiddled by our snares,
And when the brass bulled forth
A blare fit to horn over
Jericho two bars sooner
Than Joshua's harsh measures,
They still had the nerve to stare.

By the last lost chord, our director
Looked older and soberer.
No doubt, in his mind's ear
Some band somewhere
In some Music of some Sphere
Was striking a note as pure
As the wishes of Franz Schubert,
But meanwhile here we were:
A lesson in everything minor,
Decomposing our first composer.

My Father's Garden

On his way to the open hearth where white-hot steel
Boiled against furnace walls in wait for his lance
To pierce the fireclay and set loose demons
And dragons in molten tons, blazing
Down to the huge satanic caldrons,
Each day he would pass the scrapyard, his kind of garden.

In rusty rockeries of stoves and brake drums,
In grottoes of sewing machines and refrigerators,
He would pick flowers for us: small gears and cogwheels
With teeth like petals, with holes for anthers,
Long stalks of lead to be poured into toy soldiers,
Ball bearings as big as grapes to knock them down.

He was called a melter. He tried to keep his brain
From melting in those tyger-mouthed mills
Where the same steel reappeared over and over
To be reborn in the fire as something better
Or worse: cannons or cars, needles or girders,
Flagpoles, swords, or plowshares.

But it melted. His classical learning ran
Down and away from him, not burning bright.
His fingers culled a few cold scraps of Latin
And Greek, *magna sine laude,* for crosswords
And brought home lumps of tin and sewer grills
As if they were his ripe prize vegetables.

My Fire

In the cave under our house
I tended the fire: a furnace
Where black fossils of ferns
And swamp-shaking dinosaurs
Would burn through the cold mornings
If I shook the dying and dead
Ashes down through the grate
And, with firetongs, hauled out clinkers
Like the vertebrae of monsters.

I made my magic there,
Not the bloody charms of hunters,
Not shamans or animals
Painted on damp walls,
But something from fire. My father
Tended huge rows of fires
And burned with them all day,
Sometimes all evening, all night
In a steelmill, brought fire home
On his face and his burnt skin
And slept, glowing dark red.

My fire made steam in coils
And pipes and radiators
Poured from the steel he made
Somewhere I'd only seen
Far off, the burning mountains
Where God kept His true flame
To Himself, melting and turning
Blood-colored ore to pigs
And men to something stranger.

My spirit would swell and sing
Inside those pipes, would knock
And rattle to be let out,
Would circle through walls and floors,
Turn back to water and fall
To the fire again, turn white,
Rise hissing in every room
Against the windows to grow
Fronds and bone-white flowers,
All ice in a frozen garden.

The Best Slow Dancer

Under the sagging clotheslines of crepe paper
By the second string of teachers and wallflowers
In the school gym across the key through the glitter
Of mirrored light three-second rule forever
Suspended you danced with her the best slow dancer
Who stood on tiptoe who almost wasn't there
In your arms like music she knew just how to answer
The question mark of your spine your hand in hers
The other touching that place between her shoulders
Trembling your countless feet lightfooted sure
To move as they wished wherever you might stagger
Without her she turned in time she knew where you were
In time she turned her body into yours
As you moved from thigh to secrets to breast yet never
Where you would be for all time never closer
Than your cheek against her temple her ear just under
Your lips that tried all evening long to tell her
You weren't the worst one not the boy whose mother
Had taught him to count to murmur over and over
One slide two slide three slide now no longer
The one in the hallway after class the scuffler
The double clubfoot gawker the mouth breather
With the wrong haircut who would never kiss her
But see her dancing off with someone or other
Older more clever smoother dreamier
Not waving a sister somebody else's partner
Lover while you went floating home through the air
To lie down lighter than air in a moonlit shimmer
Alone to whisper yourself to sleep remember.

Looking for Nellie Washington

My job in a hard time
Was to bring those people down
To the small loan man
For a mouth-to-mouth discussion
When they'd fallen far behind
Like Nellie Washington
Who lived up a street across
An alley at the top
Of a crooked stairway through
A fence in a side yard
High-stepping down concrete
To a drain behind a basement
Garage you know by the cans
Against the incinerator.

When I finally seemed to be
Somewhere I asked somebody
Or other whereabouts
Is Nellie Washington living
Somehow around near dark
Any more the manager
Would dearly like to see her
Immediately at the latest
Or at least sooner
To talk if possible
In person the whole thing over
On the telephone tomorrow.

Then nobody I could name
Would say she headed south
Or north to a neighborhood
Next door to a home far away
In bed going to work

In school after the wreck
On the road to the hospital
Except for an hour ago
Yesterday just last week
She was downstairs in the front
Of the back in number something
As far as they could forget
To say what she looked like.

In back of the front I almost
Saw through a crack in a door
A shape moving beyond
A strip of stained wallpaper
Banana-peeled to the floor
Like a window shade unwound
To the edge of a curled carpet
Something maybe like her
One black hand turned light
At the frame to flip good-bye
A moment before it faded
Away shut gone for good
Forever like her credit.

Does her bad-account-chaser's card
Wherever it went still say
Nothing Nothing Nobody
Called Called Again Nellie
Washington where are you now
That your better business number
Was up to be disconnected
Down in black against white
On the dotted line of the Man
When you didn't come on in
Come out wherever you were
Supreme as mysterious
Unlimited beyond me
As God the National Debt
With interest so long forgiven
As I owe you I quit.

My Father's Football Game

He watched each TV game for all he was worth, while swaying
Off guard or around end, his jaw
Off-center. He made each tackle
Personally, took it personally if the runner broke through
To a broken field. He wanted that hotshot
Down, up and around and down
Hard, on the ground, now, no matter which team was which.

Star backs got all the cheers. Their names came rumbling, roaring
Out of grandstands from the loud mouths
Of their fathers. He'd show them
How it felt out cold for a loss, to be speared, the pigskin
Fumbled and turned over. Man
To man he would smile then
For the linemen, *his* team, the scoreless iron men getting even.

But if those flashy legs went flickering out of the clutches
Of the last tackler into the open
Past anyone's goal line, he would stand
For a moment of silence, bent, then take his bitter cup
To the kitchen, knowing time
Had been called for something sweeter
Than any victory: he would settle down to his dream game

Against Jim Thorpe and the Carlisle Indians for Washington
& Jefferson, buddy, that Great Year
By George Nineteen Sixteen
In mud, sweat, and sleet, in padding thinner than chain mail,
With immortal guts and helmets
Flying, the Savages versus the Heroes
By failing light in a Götterdämmerung, Nothing to Nothing.

My Father in the Basement

Something had gone wrong down in the basement.
Something important needed rearranging
Or shaping up down there like the neat shadows
He kept in the coal bin and under the workbench.
But when he went to find it, he couldn't find it.

None of the fuses had blown as dark as storms
At their tiny portholes. Nothing was on fire
But the fire in the furnace, and nothing was frozen
But the humming freezer and the concrete floor
And the hands he'd poured it with, now cold and hard.

Had his mother sent him there to fetch crab apples,
Spicy and gold, or piccalilli for supper?
Was that his father shouting and then turning
A deaf ear to his answer? It was cold
And hard to remember why he wasn't working.

So he lay down on the floor, doing things right
The first time because nothing was worth doing
Unless he did it himself. There was no use
In calling strangers if something was out of order
Because if he couldn't fix it, nobody could.

My Father's Ghost

If you count nine stars and nine stones, then look into an empty room,
you'll see a ghost.
　—*Midwestern folk belief*

I counted them, and now I look through the door
Into the empty room where he was, where nine stars
Have failed to conjure him under a ceiling
Presiding over nothing except a floor
And four walls without windows, where nine stones
Have failed to call him up from the netherworld
To tell me of his cruel unnatural murder.

He stays as invisible as other souls
In either world. I have to imagine him
In this interior without natural light,
Recall him burned by splashing steel each shift
Of his unnatural life, his thigh broken
To an Oedipal limp, his eyes half-blinded
By staring into the pits of open hearths,
His memory put to sleep, his ears deafened
By the slamming of drop forges and the roar
Of fire as bright as the terrible hearts of stars,
Of fire that would melt stones. He won't come back
At anyone's bidding in his hard hat of a helmet,
His goggles up like a visor, but I dream him
Returning unarmed, unharmed. Words, words. I hold
My father's ghost in my arms in his dark doorway.

Elegy for My Mother

She heard the least footfall, the least sigh
Or whisper beyond a door, the turning
Of a page in a far room, the most distant birdsong,

Even a slight wind when it was barely
Beginning: she would wait at a window
For someone to come home, for someone sleeping

To stir and waken, for someone far away
To tell her anything she could murmur
Word for word for years, for those close by

To be alive and well in stories she loved
To listen to all day, where life after life
Kept happening to others, but not to her,

And it was no surprise to forget herself
One morning, to misplace wherever she was,
Whoever she was, and become a ghostly wonder

Who would never wonder why it didn't matter
If no one listened to her or whether
She was here or there or even somewhere

Or why it felt so easy not to linger
In the doorway saying hello, good-bye, or remember
Me, but simply to turn and disappear.

In the Dream House

My father, having changed
From his comfortable well-worn
Once-in-a-lifetime tweeds,
Which he never owned, wears now
As the man of the dream house
A flower in his silk lapel
And stands poised by my mother
Who is radiantly younger
In the dress he never bought her
And kisses her longingly
And lingeringly, not fearful
Of heaven or the neighbors,
As if he'd loved her before
The taxi, the orchestra,
The champagne, and the private laughter,
Which they never called or heard
Or opened or uttered,
And they're holding each other
Not with self-contained arms
But with one accord, one impulse
Of uncontrollable joy
Over what could be their lives,
And there in his firelit den
He looks at her and smiles
Out of pride with open eyes,
Which he no longer has.

Their Bodies

To the students of anatomy at Indiana University

That gaunt old man came first, his hair as white
As your scoured tables. Maybe you'll recollect him
By the scars of steelmill burns on the backs of his hands,
On the nape of his neck, on his arms and sinewy legs,
And her by the enduring innocence
Of her face, as open to all of you in death
As it would have been in life: she would memorize
Your names and ages and pastimes and hometowns
If she could, but she can't now, so remember her.

They believed in doctors, listened to their advice,
And followed it faithfully. You should treat them
One last time as they would have treated you.
They had been kind to others all their lives
And believed in being useful. Remember somewhere
Their son is trying hard to believe you'll learn
As much as possible from them, as *he* did,
And will do your best to learn politely and truly.

They gave away the gift of those useful bodies
Against his wish. (They had their own ways
Of doing everything, always.) If you're not certain
Which ones are theirs, be gentle to everybody.

THREE

Stump Speech

This is the bark, which is always dead.

This is the phloem, which only lives
To carry sunlight down from the leaves,
Then dies into bark, which is always dead.

This is the cambium. Every year
It thickens another ring to wear
And swells the phloem, which only lives
To carry sunlight down from the leaves,
Then dies into bark, which is always dead.

This is the xylem. It lifts the rain
Two hundred feet from root to vein
Out of a cambium well. Each year
It thickens another ring to wear
And swells the phloem, which only lives
To carry sunlight down from the leaves,
Then dies into bark, which is always dead.

This is the heartwood, once locked in
As hard as iron by pitch and resin
Inside the xylem that lifted rain
Two hundred feet from root to vein,
Now soft as cambium out to where
It thickened a final ring to wear,
Then shrank like the phloem that swelled with life
Called down like sunlight from each leaf
Behind the bark, which is always dead.

And this is the stump I stand beside,
Once tall, now short as the day it died
And gray as driftwood, its heartwood eaten
By years of weather, its xylem rotten
And only able to hold the rain
One cold inch (roots withered and gone)
In a shallow basin, a cracked urn
Whose cambium and phloem now learn
To carry nothing down to the dark
Inside the broken shell of the bark
But a dream of a tree forever dead.

And this is the speech that grew instead.

An Address to Weyerhaeuser,
the Tree-Growing Company

After miles of stumps and slash and the once-buried endeavors
Of roots, all dozer-bladed to their logical ends, the clear-cut
Ends finally at a stand of firs near a creek, and for an hour
I've listened to what's left of the winter wrens
Claiming the little they can for territory.

(Which isn't much. And I'm too mad to be lyrical about it,
Lacking their grace, their fearlessness, their ingenuity.
Let somebody else do it: one of the most beautiful songs
In North America, a long, wild, ringing melody,
Says *The Complete Fieldguide to American Wildlife*. It lasts
For seven seconds with sixteen distinct notes and sixteen stops
Per second, an amazing 112 notes, says *Life Histories*
Of North American Birds. Our machines can barely track them.)

One comes to scout me where I sit on the last stump
Before the forest holds out its dark-green light again.
He sings, watching me. There's no use trying to say
What the music is like, cascading out of this short-tailed genius
Smaller than a mouse. Another answers and another,
Distinct though distant. I catch a glimpse of one through glasses
Down by the creek. Being as scientific as the next-to-last man,
I mark the spot and measure it off on the deep soft forest floor
(No rhapsodic passages about licorice fern and running pine and moss)
As clumsily as a moon-walker. His voice was carrying
Clearly and easily five hundred feet and could have reached
        further,
But I'll stay reasonably sober: this tiny groundling,
This incredibly gifted ounce was moving and reclaiming
A hemisphere of June air weighing nine tons.

Mr. Weyerhaeuser, your fallers and heavy thinkers made this possible.
I realize June is a distracting month: you must trap and kill
All those ravenous black bears whose berries haven't ripened
And who maul and gnaw a few of your billions of saplings
And you're looking forward to spraying the already dying
Tussock moths again, regardless of our expense, regardless
Of what else may be trying to live under the branches,
But for a moment consider *Troglodytes troglodytes*, this wren
Who has never forged a treaty or plotted a war
Or boasted of trying to serialize massacre after massacre
Or managed a forest or suffered the discomfort of an obituary
Listing credits in fraternal and charitable parlays
And other safe bets: he's moving a greater weight
Of living and dead matter daily than all your logging crews.
This creature smaller than your opposable thumb
And much more subtle is singing all day
In the woods you haven't clear-cut yet. Each song
Lasts seven seconds and forever. Think what you might manage
To move if you could sing or even listen.

The Shape

The seed falls, lies still through rain,
Lies covered by snow through its after-ripening,
Then swells in the lengthening days
And bursts, and the primary root
Turns down to make its way
Through the newly dead and the long dead,
And the lateral roots spread wide
To brace for the lifting-up and the opening
Of the caul-pale embryo to the light,
And the roots deepen and darken, and the stem
Hardens and stiffens and lifts higher
The first unfolding leaves and the first branches,
And the roots embrace themselves, embrace stones,
Embrace the earth that holds them, sending their dream
High into the storms of the moon and wind,
The storms of the sun and stars for years.

What falls against the mind and lies still?—
Lies covered and cold, yet ripens,
Spreads down through a wealth of the half-remembered
And the forgotten, the unknown, to a deeper darkness,
To transparent eyes, to the ends of fingers, then raises
Into a storm this branched unreasoning shape?

Three Ways of a River

Sometimes, without a murmur, the river chooses
    The clearest channels, the easy ways
Downstream, dividing at islands equally, smoothly,
And meeting itself once more on the far side
    In a gathering of seamless eddies
That blend so well, no ripples rise to break

Into light like fingerlings taking their first mayflies
    Or, again, it will rush at overhangs
And blunder constantly against bare stone,
Against some huge implacable rock face
    To steepen and plunge, spring wide, go white,
And be dashed in tatters of spray, revolved and scattered

Like rain clouds pouring forward against a cliff
    In an endless storm of its own making,
While calmly a foot away lies the shape all water
Becomes if it flows aside into a pool,
    As still as the rock that holds it, as level
As if held cold to drink in these two hands.

The Excursion of the Speech and Hearing Class

They had come to see the salmon lunging and leaping
Up the white spillway, but the water was empty.
Now one young girl lingers behind the others,
And slowly, her thin arms held out from her sides,
Alone on the riverbank, she begins to dance.

Her body moves as the salmon would have moved
In place, holding that place in a soundless calm
Under a soundless frenzy of surfaces
Against a current only she remembers
To welcome, to break through, to gather again.

The wind and the river pulse against her face
And under her feet. She listens to what they know
And moves her lips to find the mouth of the river
And the mouth of the slow wind against her mouth.
The source of the river and the source of the wind

Have taken her breath away. But the others come
Shaking their fingers, opening and closing
Their mouths, to take her back to another silence.

Driftwood

From its burial at sea, a gray-white forest
Has come to Dungeness Spit to lie ashore:
Whole trees, their bark long-lost, their roots clutching
Only the wind, their jumbled branches
Smooth-sided schools of fish.

Not one of the thousands, thousands strewn for miles
Across and among each other, gnarled or straight
Or broken, level, slanted or half-buried
In sand, not one though dead and left
For dead gestures of storms,

For masters of sea wrack done with dying now
In the salted calm of knots and rings and veins,
In every cell still held out to the light
Or the rain, having no more to do
With stretching and letting fall,

Not one though leafless, the green gone, cast away
And stranded here like the bones of forgotten seasons,
The bones of the dying gods of moving water
And weather, under our eyes or fingers
Not one not beautiful.

FOUR

On Motel Walls

Beyond the foot of the bed: a seascape whose ocean,
Under the pummeling of a moon the shape and shade
Of a wrecking ball, is breaking into slabs
Against a concrete coast. Next to the closet:
A landscape of pasty mountains no one could climb
Or fall from, beyond whose sugary grandeur
Lies Flatland, a blankness plastered on plasterboard.
And over the bed: a garden in the glare
Of shadowless noon where flowerheads burst more briefly
And emptily and finally than fireworks.

For hours, I've been a castaway on that shore
By that fake water where nothing was ever born,
Where the goddess of beauty sank. I've flopped on those slopes
Where no one on earth could catch a breath worth breathing,
And I've been caught in that garden
Where the light is neither waves nor particles
But an inorganic splatter without a source.

Tonight, what's in the eye of this beholder
Is less and less and all the ways I can go
Dead wrong myself through the quick passing
Of sentences: tomorrow, I may be staring
Straight in the face of the hanging judge of my future
Who'll read me with the deadpan of a jailer
Before a search, a lock-down, and lights out.
I'll do hard time all night inside these walls
In my mind's eye, a transient facing a door
That says, *Have you forgotten anything
Of value? Have you left anything behind?*

Applying for a Loan with the Help of the
Dictionary of Occupational Titles

> *You're a what?*
>   *—question from a credit manager*

In my other lives, I've been a sheepskin pickler,
A bowling-ball engraver, a feather washer,
Banana dispatcher, and wild cherry dipper.
I've been a bologna lacer and beeswax bleacher.
I've balanced fans, dried germs, and dipped balloons,
Served as a bellyman and a skull grinder
And saved my bacon once as a butt presser.

I've tackled even more mysterious Labors:
I've been a burning foreman, an apron scratcher,
Bar creaser, chill man, backside polisher,
Flyaway clerk, head chiseler, lingo cleaner,
Crotch joiner, hardness tester, and beat-out boy,
So don't go thinking, because I say I'm a poet,
Sir, I don't know serious work pays off.

Poem about Breath

A memory of Elizabeth Bishop, 1950

She was at work on a poem about breath.
She asked what punctuation might be strongest
For catching her breath, for breath catching
Halfway in her throat, between her straining breastbone
And her tongue, the bubbly catching of asthma.

She didn't care for ellipses or blank spaces.
Would a double colon work? Or Dickinson dashes?
It wouldn't be right for breath to have full stops.
It *does* go on, though people with trouble breathing
Think about it, and breathe, and think about it.

They think too many times of clearing the air
They have to breathe, about the air already
Down there in their lungs, not going out
On time, in time, and when it's finally gone,
Not coming back to the place longing to keep it.

Each breath turns into a problem like a breath
In a poem that won't quite fit, giving the wrong
Emphasis to a feeling or breaking the rhythm
In a clumsy way, where something much more moving
Could happen to keep that poem moving and breathing.

She said as a child she'd learned *one* different style
Of breathing, and her eyelids lowered and darkened.
She bowed her full, firm, pale, remarkable face,
Then solemnly lifted it and opened her mouth,
Stuck out her curled-back tongue and, while it quivered,

Unfolded it slowly, balancing near the end
A half-inch bubble of saliva, gleaming.
With her lightest breath, she puffed it, and it floated
Through late summer light along the workroom window
All the way to the sill before it broke.

Then she bent over and over, choking with laughter.

Catching the Big One at Lone Lake

A memory of Richard Hugo, 1956

From the rowboat, loosely tied
To a broken dock, he glared
At the enemy in the distance:
The other fishermen catching
The brightest living silver
For themselves. For him, nothing.

He'd expected nothing, he said,
As usual. What else was new?
It was just like writing poems:
Dumb luck sometimes. He glanced
Up shore to a weedy house
Where nothing was waiting.

And then he hooked the lunker.
As he rose to his bare feet
In its honor, it rose too,
Wildly, an outsized rainbow
In rainbows, whose highest leap
Sent it whirligigging sideways

To the dock where it fishtailed
Head first down through a hole
In the planks to splash once more
Out of sight. And almost sinking
Both of us, ankle deep
Among empties and sandwiches,

Deep-sixing his rod and reel,
He went after it, scrambled and slammed
Down in a belly-flop
Across loose rotten boards,
Guided the taut line clear
Of snags, then hand over hand,

Slowly, against each change
Of direction, each quick lunge,
Brought up into the light
(As gaping and round-eyed
And astonished as *he* was) the one
That didn't get away.

Eulogy for Richard Hugo (1923–82)

We both wore masks. Mine over my mouth
Was there to catch each word, each dangerous breath
Before it reached the man sitting in bed
And found its way through his defenseless blood.
His mask was a royal bruise across his chest
(Where one lung labored, labored hard as Christ
To cure the marrow that had turned against him)
And the swollen flesh of a face, once lean and handsome,
Now stretched past guilt and fear, past innocence
And courage into a skin-tight radiance.

While blood hung on a scaffold, dripping warm
And slow to its cold future in his arm,
He talked of jobs and money and old games,
Of letters and love, good humor and bad dreams,
Of what he'd learned, in pain, about his lives,
Of struggles between his better and bitter halves.

For thirty years I'd known a starving child
Inside him, tough and subtle, shrewd and squalid,
Who shared his body, glaring through his eyes
And balking at the cost of wretchedness.
Outside, he wore a life intensely human
And over that, at times, like a mad shaman,
The skulls of enemies and the skins of beasts,
Tatters of beggar boys and family ghosts—
Sacred disguises. "What I do is me"
Became for him "What I seem, we all may be."

These struggling selves made poems, did without
The gibberish of God, grudge-matching wit,
The urge to pose or maunder, prattle or preach,
And sang blunt beautiful American speech
In voices none of us had heard before,
Whose burden was "We can grow up through fear."

He spent his days in search of a hometown
Where he could be class hero and class clown,
Unknown and famous, friendly and alone:
Wearing his old school colors, the gray and white
Of ashes, he lies there now, its laureate.

Elegy while Pruning Roses

What saint strained so much,
Rose on such lopped limbs to a new life?
—*Theodore Roethke*

I've weeded their beds, put down manure and bark dust.
Now comes the hard part: theoretically
It has to be done, or they spend their blooming season
In a tangle of flowerless, overambitious arms.
So here go pruning shears in spite of the thorns
That kept off browsers for all the millennia
Before some proto-dreamer decided roses
Were beautiful or smelled their unlikely promise.

Reluctantly I follow the book and stunt them
In the prescribed shapes, but throwing cuttings away
Over the fence to die isn't easy.
They hang onto my gloves and won't let go,
Clutching and backlashing as if fighting
To stay in the garden, but I don't have time or patience
To root them in sand, transplant them, and no room
In an overcrowded plot, even supposing
They could stand my lame midhusbandry.
So into limbo with all these potential saints.

Already the ladybugs, their black-dotted orange
Houses always on fire, are climbing for aphids,
And here come leaf-rollers, thrips and mildew
To have their ways. I've given up poison:
These flowers are on their own for the spring and summer.
But watching the blood-red shoots fade into green
And buds burst to an embarrassing perfection,
I'll cut bouquets of them and remember
The dying branches tumbling downhill together.

Ted, you told me once there were days and days
When you *had* to garden, to get your hands
Down into literal dirt and bury them
Like roots to remind yourself what you might do
Or be next time, with luck. I've searched for that mindless
Ripeness and found it. Later, some of these flowers
Will go to the bedside of the woman I love.
The rest are for you, who weren't cut off in your prime
But near the end of a long good growing season
Before your first frostbitten buds.
You knew where roots belonged, what mysterious roses
Come from and were meant for: thanks,
Apology, praise, celebration, wonder,
And love, in memory of the flourishing dead.

The Death of the Moon

Through the long death of the moon, we drank her light
As slowly as snow-melt, bearing her funeral
Against the turn of the earth by nights like flares
As she fell westward, trailing a torn shroud
Across the mountains, over the ashen water.

Our feet washed pale as shell, we faltered
After her, naming all she could answer,
But she turned her cold, lopsided face
Farther away than we could follow.

She shrank to half a skull,
Sinking as if to sleep
At the salt edge of her grave.

Then her white knife,
Her closing eyelid.

Her darkness.

The Astronomer's Apprentice

Some dark shadows were soon noticed crossing the Sun, and afterwards some light streaks . . . their frequency first and then their uniformity of direction . . . indicating that an unusual phenomenon was in progress. . . .
—summary of a letter from Mysore Province, India, Royal Astronomical Society, Monthly Notices, 1870

Observing the noon sun over Bangalore
Through a five-inch equatorial refractor,
Professor A. S. Herschel's assistant saw
Odd shadows move across that circle of fire
And beyond its borders where, against the sky
Like streams of meteors, they turned luminous.

Rubbing his eyes, he ruled out sparks and birds,
Then made his notes: *Motion irregular*
Like particles suspended in crosscurrents;
Their number anything short of infinite;
Distance uncertain; spectrum solar; brightness
Diminishing as they leave the edge of the disc;

Their form like half-moons sailing diameter
Forward or edgeways; sometimes almost stellar,
Distinct and brilliant; at others, double crescents
Crossbarred, trailing winglike appendages.
In Professor Herschel's absence, he beamed with joy
And traced these mysteries to the brim of evening.

He saw his fortune there in a gold shower
Bearing his name with other great dead lucky
Stargazers who had brought new wonders to light,
Who'd fixed their positions with cartographers
And now lay scattered along the bright ecliptic
Like gods and heroes drawn into constellations.

That night he even dreamed the envious demons
That ruled the world were driven by Lord Vishnu
(The All-Pervader on his giant bird)
To dance a lament on fire across the heavens
Forever, and he alone, like a favorite prince
Among earthlings, had been chosen as a witness.

All the next day he marked time with his fame
And tracked the procession north into a dazzling
Pavilion raised for a Lord of Astronomers.
On the third day, there fell at Hyderabad
Three hundred miles to the north a cloud of locusts
That ravaged everything green under the sun.

Lament for the Nonswimmers

They never feel they can be well in the water,
Can come to rest, that their bodies are light.
When they reach out, their cupped hands hesitate:
What they wanted runs between their fingers.
Their fluttering, scissoring legs sink under.

Their bones believe in heaviness, their ears
Shake out the cold invasion of privacy,
Their eyes squeeze shut. Each breath,
Only half air, is too breathtaking.
The dead man's float seems strictly for dead men.

They stand in the shallows, their knees touching,
Their feet where they belong in the sand.
They wade as carefully as herons, but hope for nothing
Under the surface, that wilderness
Where eels and sharks slip out of their element.

Those who tread water and call see their blurred eyes
Turn distant, not away from a sky's reflection
As easy to cross as the dependable earth
But from a sight as blue as drowned men's faces.
They splash ashore, pretending to feel buoyant.

The Naval Trainees Learn How to Jump Overboard

The last trainees are climbing the diving tower
As slowly as they dare, their fingers trembling
On the wet rungs, bare feet reluctantly
Going one step higher, one more, too far
Above the water waiting to take them in.

They stand on top, knees slightly buckled, nowhere
To put their hands, all suddenly thinking how
Good it's always been to be braced up
By something, anything, but ready to be let down
By their loud instructor thirty feet below.

They are the last ones learning how to jump
Feet-first into the swimming pool, to windward
From an imagined ship (in case of drift or fire),
Their ankles crossed, their loose life jackets held
Down with one hand, their noses pinched with the other.

They pause at the edge. Only one second away
From their unsupported arches, the surface glitters,
Looking too solid, too jagged and broken,
A place strictly for sinking, no place to go.
Each has his last split-second second thoughts.

Others are treading water, hooting and whistling
Abandon Ship and General Alarm,
But these stare toward the emptiest of horizons.
Upright, blue-lipped, no longer breathing, already
Drowned, they commit their bodies to the deep.

Canticle for Xmas Eve

O holy night as it was in the beginning
Under silent stars for the butchering of sheep
And shepherds, is now and ever shall be, night,

How still we see thee lying under the angels
In twisted wreckage, squealing, each empty eye-slit
Brimful of light as it was in the beginning

Of our slumber through the sirens wailing and keening
Over the stained axe and the shallow grave
That was, is now, and ever shall be, night

Of the night-light, chain and deadlatch by the bolt
Slammed home, the spell of thy deep and dreamless
Everlasting sleep as it was in the beginning

Of the bursting forth of bright arterial blossoms
From the pastures of our hearts to the dark streets
Shining what is and shall be for this night

Of bludgeons and hopes, of skulls and fears laid open
To the mercies of our fathers burning in heaven,
O little town of bedlam in the beginning
Of the end as it was, as it is to all, good night.

Your Fortune: A Cold Reading

When a fortune-teller knows nothing in advance about a client, he/she is forced to give a "cold reading," a fortune applying to almost anyone, but sounding very personal.

Say nothing revealing. You needn't tell
Anything about yourself or what you suppose
You are or were or what you're going to be.
Give away no secrets. While you sit there, trusting
Nothing you hear, you will hear your fortune.

This is your lucky day, but you don't know
Quite where to turn. Your life is approaching
A sudden climax, but making up your mind
Has always been hard for you. This lack
Of confidence has lost you chance after chance.

Too much of the strongest and most beautiful
Stays hidden in you, unused, neglected:
Your influential ease, your powers of persuasion,
And that gift of inborn charm (through no fault
Of your own) are largely unknown to those around you.

And you deserve far better than that. Now someone
Is coming toward you, older, gray-haired, dark-eyed,
To tell you wonderful news, but you won't listen.
Another person, shorter, pale-eyed, fair-haired,
Is lying to you, and until you know that fact

Your future is shadowed. You stay faithful in love
As long as your love is faithful, but you feel
Dissatisfied, unfulfilled. This nervousness
Is the pivot of your problems. Here at the turning
Point of your life, you must finally choose.

You are more sensitive and romantic now
Than you have ever been. You need love and attention,
But in spite of all you say or do, no matter
What you wear or how you groom your body,
Your heart, your mind, and what you trust is your soul

Feel strangely empty. You have someone only
Halfway into your life, half in strange dreams,
Who will not tell you whether you're close to parting
Or coming closer together. A would-be lover
Is waiting for you, but may soon give up hope.

You gave in once to the conventional world,
Taking its orders, obeying its rules, but lately
Because of your impulsive, heart-led nature,
You have begun to change and have suffered for it
From the tongues of neighbors and friendly hypocrites.

But soon you will learn to trust your own good judgment.
You will live long, be wealthier and wiser.
You don't know how unusual you are.
If you could have the answer to one question
Now, truly, secretly, what would it be?

The Calm

Drifting and mimicking the loss of the wind
With a loss of mind,
Left slack-sailed here in the sea, doing nothing at all
For days, we begin
Taking our lives uneasily. Only the daylight
And the cracked chronometer
Are moving. Though we turn away from the sun
Or rise under the moon
As if we were earth and tide, the rest is stillness.
If we broke our silence,
This palpable air would ripple obediently,
But our voices falter.
They melt on the sea, as brief as glints of starlight.
On the deep dry land
Why did we never think of the miles and miles
Under us, holding us?
Above half-leagues of water, we think of little
Else than how deeply
The two of us might sink, turning to food
For the thoughts of others.
We could have stayed on firmament, on a desert
Where water waves good-bye,
Good-bye, and vanishes, a plain where it flows
On its own slight journeys,
Or on mountains where we could watch it frozen, toppling
(Instead of us) down cliffsides.
But here we huddle, surrounded. From miles below,
Now, come the monsters
Toward the glassy calm around us, uncoiling,
Lifting kelp-ragged
Slime-scaled snag-toothed cold impossible heads,
Eyes filled to the brim

With blankness, breaching and hulking, slewing toward us
Where we drift like lures.
Though they come closer, closer, blurred in the dark,
They never strike, never
Loom, ravenous, never thrash the surface
To break this mirror.

Reading the Sky

Look, love, the sky is full again, as full as our sails.
Not being weather-wise, we read the baffling
Language of that sky
Slowly and doubtfully. Some skillful mariner might know
The signs like the palms of our hands and tell us
What we must do today
To be ready for tomorrow, but we murmur the names
Of clouds as if they were friendly enemies
Not meant to be trusted
To go where they should go or not to disguise themselves
Suddenly in different masks and colors.
The sky reminds us
Of our unpredictable minds: irresolute, inconstant,
Oracular, full of a mysterious music,
Barren, well- and ill-tempered.
Though we can't make it reveal its futures or our fortunes,
Here on the crests of waves that move us and move us
We can pay it honor:
We know its blues and reds, like our bodies, are born of dust,
Its whites and grays mere vaporings, its blackness
Concealed by dazzle,
But all this broken beauty of cloud-shapes, the endless
Promises and the unrepeatable gestures
Of light, omens, high masses,
Each shred, each smattering of each flamboyant skyscape
Have numbed our language into a mawkish grandeur.
Though it may look absolute
For death to those beaten by storms, it can never be ugly
And never meager or miserly, always lavish
With unself-conscious praise
Of itself, even when empty. Let others people it
With hosts of maladroit gods, benign or vengeful,
Flinging stones or manna:

What it really is is gift and weapon enough. Though Heaven
Be lost or strayed or stolen, we have the heavens
Instead to venture beneath
From beginning to end, and though we come to the end of the earth,
The waterfall of the vanishing ocean, the dropping-off place,
We bear these heavens with us.

Landfall

Our boat aground, we bring slow feet ashore, and they sink
But not in sand alone. They keep believing
In the sea: they rise
And fall, not understanding. They won't agree with the land
Or each other, stumbling sideways in memory
Of the waves now breaking
Calmly and raggedly behind us. We're upright, and we seem
To stand, and we turn like worlds half free of the world,
Small moons spinning near
Our mother, earthbound but dazed by distance. Have we come home?
Is this where we were born? Is this where it was
All along, this place
Where, again, we must learn to walk? We wallow from the water
Like our hesitant helpless curious ancestors,
Taking our first taste
Of the different air and kneeling awash as if to pray
For trust in what holds us up less yieldingly
After a sea change,
No longer buoyant, bearing the burden of inescapable
Heaviness among strangers who are already
Shyly coming toward us,
Asking what seem to be questions in an unknown language.
Is it what we've always asked ourselves? *Who are you?*
Can you be trusted?
What do you want? They hold their hands behind them, hiding
Flowers or knives. Love, remember not caring
Whether this was the end of us
When we set out, embarking on new lives with nothing
To lose but our names? Now all turns nameless again
For us who must love to learn
Once more how to point at the trees and birds and animals
We see around us, even our own hearts,
Naming, renaming them.

FIVE

For a Woman Who Doubted the Power of Love

Didn't I say the sun would cross the sky
Like a burning stone
And, like a burnt stone, fall in the evening
To light the pathway
Of the huge red stone of the moon rising
For our eyes only?
Didn't I say the moon would fade and leave us
Pale as our faces
Here at the end of night as we lie together
Under the drifting snow?
Didn't I say all snow would turn to water,
Each drop a flower,
That the sun would rise as molten as always
In time with birdsong
By the light of our moving arms in the morning?
My love, listen and learn
Once more how I did all this by the power
Of your heart and my heart.
How could the sky and these falling starlit leaves
Catch fire without us?

Falling Asleep in a Garden

All day the bees have come to the garden.
They hover, swivel in arcs and, whirling, light
On stamens heavy with pollen, probe and revel
Inside the yellow and red starbursts of dahlias
Or cling to lobelia's blue-white mouths
Or climb the speckled trumpets of foxgloves.

My restless eyes follow their restlessness
As they plunge bodily headfirst into treasure,
Gold-fevered among these horns of plenty.
They circle me, a flowerless patch
With nothing to offer in the way of sweetness
Or light against the first omens of evening.

Some, even now, are dying at the end
Of their few weeks, some being born in the dark,
Some simply waiting for life, but some are dancing
Deep in their hives, telling the hungry
The sun will be that way, the garden this far:
This is the way to the garden. They hum at my ear.

And I wake up, startled, seeing the early
Stars beginning to bud in constellations.
The bees have gathered somewhere like petals closing
For the coming of the cold. The silhouette
Of a sphinx moth swerves to drink at a flowerhead.
The night-blooming moon opens its pale corolla.

The Orchard of the Dreaming Pigs

As rosy as sunsets over their cloudy hocks, the pigs come flying
Evening by evening to light in the fruit trees,
Their trotters firm on the bent boughs, their wings
All folding down for the dark as they eat and drowse,
Their snouts snuffling a comfortable music.

At dawn, as easily as the light, they lift
Their still-blessed souse and chitlings through the warming air,
Not wedging their way like geese, but straggling
And curling in the sunrise, rising, then soaring downward
To the bloody sties, their breath turned sweet as apples.

Waking Up in a Garden

We wake together, discovering the garden
Has gone to sleep around us, the sky dead black.
We've nearly forgotten
The when and where of love that brought us here
And left us near sundown, the why and how of our lives
At the familiar strange beginning of night.

The moths are hovering at the shadows of flowers,
Engrossed by their blurred labors, some zigzagging
Wildly, cross-purposefully,
And some in whorls like nebulae, constellations
Unstrung from the belt of their small zodiac
To fade and waver down into the grass.

And sweeping by, the bats are taking others
Silently and carefully into silence.
A nighthawk, the backswept
Outlines of its wings dark crescent moons,
Swoops near again and again. The moths vanish,
Reappear and vanish, die, spin back transformed,

And we lie under this feast like part of it,
Not wishing ourselves the sure wings of the hunters
But, lighter than feathers,
The baffling erratic uncontrollably crooked
Night-bearing gifted star-marked wings of the hunted
Whose tongues, like ours, go spiraling into sweetness.

A Woman Feeding Gulls

They cry out at the sight of her and come flying
Over the tidal flats from miles away,
Sideslipping and wheeling
In sloping gray-and-white interwoven spirals
Whose center is her
And the daily bread she casts downwind on the water
While rising to spread her arms
Like wings for the calling of still more gulls around her,
Their cries intermingling at the end of daylight
With the sudden abundance
Of this bread returning after the hungry night
And the famine of morning
And the endlessly hungry opening and closing
Of wings and arms and shore and the turning sky.

A Woman Standing in the Surf

Thigh-deep in the sea, she watches waves arriving
As if those storms
Thousands of miles away in starry spirals
Or the long upheavals
Of fire from the ocean bed or the almost breathless
Breathless baffling
Of winds by the moon had all been brought to bear
And to light on this shore
For her alone, each having known all along
Where she was waiting
And how to touch her coldly, billowing gently
Or suddenly surging
As she rises to meet them, crying out out of fear
Of her desire, in wonder
Outspreading her arms over water to welcome them
Against her, against her.

Lifesaving

Those arms stretching toward you helplessly,
Beating the waves and clutching the air,
Want to hang on, they want to hold you close,
Closer forever, not out of love
But fear of losing a way of life by drowning.

No matter how reassuringly you say
To listen and trust you, to relax and give in
To the easy water lifting you together,
That mind staring at you and at nothing
Can't understand *why* it should stop screaming.

One hand is suddenly seizing you, half-strangling,
And one wild crook of an arm is locking
Around your head, and that mind is losing its mind.
Not losing yours, you do what the water
Around you has done already: you give way.

You go away from the light and air, you settle
Downward as if to end the world
Of the head and heart, taking the other with you
As far down as that body will follow
Into the darkness, and it lets you go.

It rises again to the uncertain surface,
No longer thrashing, no longer grappling
Or flailing, out of its wits, but desperately calm.
It believes you now. It's lying still
While your palm is lifting it gently, almost weightless,

The face aimed at the sky, the mind once more
Seeing and listening, remembering
To believe its body can float as well as yours,
That its arms and legs can begin to move
Surely with yours toward the land of the living.

That Moment

Having swum farther than he'd known he could swim, so far
He'd stopped looking for land
And had simply gone on swimming and swimming till his arms
Slowed, exhausted,
And his legs, no longer fluttering, faltering out of time
With his heart, began
To settle slowly deeper and deeper into water
(For all he knew
Deeper than any water he'd ever crossed), that moment
His feet, instead of nothing, touch
The soft upflow of earth to bear them, and he starts breathing
Almost as if each breath
Might follow another, as if he could depend on knowing
From this breath forward
That his body, though nearly weightless, might move once more
Light-stepped, as buoyant
As light on the face of the moon, alive after all
That dying, that moment
He turns and walks toward her in a room, his love
For her that moment beginning.

A Guide to the Field

Through this wild pasture, this mile of strewn grasses,
We walk among seed crowns
Only half-formed at the beginning of summer
But already growing
Heavier with the burdens nothing will harvest
But birds and the weather,
Some (this ryegrass) like caterpillars spinning
Cocoons out of sunlight,
And some (this lavender bluegrass) a waist-high forest
Of slender fir trees,
Still others (cheatgrass, wild barley) plotted like flowerbeds
Under flights and counter-flights
Of swallows and field sparrows. Each blade, each spikelet,
Each glume and awn, each slowly
Stiffening stem, no matter what may come
In the next wind—hail or fire—
Will take its beheading, will give up this year's ghost
With less than a murmur,
And we pass beside them now, taking together
Our first strange steps
On a path that leads us down to its end in water.
Each look, the first.
Each touch of our strange fingers, the first again.
Each movement of our bodies
As strangely startling as what the swallows dare
Skimming the pond, their wingtips
Glancing, glancing again, swept-luminous crescents,
Each act of theirs
As if for us only. They show us ways to turn
Into willing lovers
Not needing to say *Yes* on this day when all questions,
Even before the asking,
Have mingled with their answers. Remember winter:
Birds gone, seeming lost,
And the grass lying down once more to pretend one death,

Dried pale and brittle
By a hard-earned hard-learned gift of seeming done
With its life. Love dies, and love
Is born at the same heart-roots in words once cold
And comfortless as a scattering
Of ashes: *All flesh is grass* meaning *Love lies down*
Mortal, immortal.

Getting Away

We had brought our love there: to a lake by a forest
And by nightfall at the firelit hearthstone lay
Together to whisper it, to become it,
To dream it. But something wanted out of the closet.

The rat-scratching began at the inner threshold,
Moved up the jamb and scratched at the lintel
And went scuffling left and right along bare walls,
Searching a way out but falling and scrabbling.

We had met life from the woods already, gray-and-white
Mouse heads peeking tremulously between floorboards,
And had heard them tip-tailing carefully from spring
To spring in the loveseat, holding their nesting ground,

And in their behalf, and in love's, had decided to live
And let live, to share the bread we'd broken
Under this roof where they were as safe from claws
As we were from new preachments and old orders.

But this was no subtle mousy deferential
Skittering. It was an unabashed declaration
Of independence by something as good as lovers
At making and having its way and getting away.

We tried pounding the door, imagining wood rats
Like city rats would have the self-regard
To quit and go into hiding and come back later
When they would have themselves to themselves like us.

But the scratches went on, not pausing, went on
And on without fear, without flinching, without shifting
To the ceiling or underfoot on whatever passage
This fellow creature had gnawed and wriggled through.

So at last with brooms and boots and the righteous courage
Of tenancy (our self-possession being
Nine points of our law) we braced ourselves
To face the tenth, having propped the porch door wide

To tempt it into the hospitality
Of the night where it would be welcome naturally
And opened the closet door, while cringing sideways,
And saw the tawny-backed slender snow-breasted weasel

Standing erect, the small paws dangling, gazing
From brooms to us more calmly than possible
And tilting a small incredibly sinuous head
And neck on its shoulderless body, slowly deciding

To let us go on being where we were
Whatever we were, whatever we meant to be,
And it bent at the baseboard and glided on all fours
Around the corner and out the door down the stairs

More smoothly and silently than the evening
Had climbed them, and disappeared into the darkness
And left us and the mice in that good house
Where nothing stirred but all of us till morning.

Our Blindness

I see you now, and now
With the sudden end of lamplight
At the bedside have lost you
For a brief while to the night
Except for the pale drift
Of the pillow beside your face
And, over your landscape,
The softly touching whiteness
Of the sheet like a bed of snow.

Now love is blind. We move
To find what we can't see
Across the strange familiar
Neighborhood of our bodies
Like the blind when a snowfall
Has muffled and smoothed away
All shapes from their feet and fingers
To make a second blindness.
We turn to all we know.

By Starlight

Now far from those harsh lights and the glare over cities, alone
By a clearing in a forest, we lie down
For the first time in our lives
Together under stars
And, keeping the earth in its place behind our backs, we stare
Upward into the ancient stream of starlight
Whose current, though it appears
To falter, to waver,
Has made its way to our eyes through barely imaginable
Down-curved ravines of space to dazzle us
With its streamers and wildfires,
Its ice-laden glitter,
The unconstellated burning rubble of godlings, outcast
And spilled from the zodiac and constantly falling
As they have always fallen
Even before eyes turned
To wonder and will go on falling whether we stay to watch
Or soon give back our small share of the spectrum
To the oldest of nights, to the expansive
Gestures of a universe
We share so pointedly: some (see there) bloomed long ago
And dimmed, yet shine through lifetimes without a source,
With no beginning left
Behind them now
To begin with, but only an ever-shortening reach of glory
That flickers in darkness. All will consume themselves
And be reborn, as we are
Here, having followed
Their example, love, as fixed and erring and fair and steadfast,
Not star-crossed yet, but truly catching them
As they slant to us past hemlocks, as rich
And clear as our silence.

For a Third Anniversary

You brought me wildflowers once, not the real ones
You'd learned and loved after school along the roadside
April by April, after the city fathers
Had cut them down—*poppies and vetch, pentstemon
And bleeding heart*—not the ones you'd gathered
For other grudging teachers who'd held your life
And your life-to-be too lightly, but words in a poem.

You set them down so gently, so carefully,
So quietly, I almost didn't notice
They were saying good-bye to me. *Cut flowers,* you said,
Rootless. Bright awkward moments already wilting.
No sweets, no charms, no dancing, you said, but words
Like flowers, *removed from life.* A lesson in loss.

Years late, into the yard behind the house
We share, I bring my answer: river stones,
Deer fern, moss, and stumps from forest floors,
Survivors of neglect and mayhem, like words.
From among them, from what seemed a barren garden
As bleak as hope, come yellow violets,
Starflowers, and wild red currant.

Downstream

We give in to the persuasions of the river, floating
Swiftly downstream as well as the leaves beside us,
Ahead of us, with little choice
Which way it may be next
That we find ourselves
One boat-length farther along, taking the rough with the smooth,
To the slackness of pools, down long, eddying riffles,
To the rush of spillways narrowing
And steepening suddenly
To white water
Where the river is leaving everything to chance and turning
Over and interrupting its own half-motions
Constantly in bursts and arches,
Mantling, spun into tendrils,
Its wild gestures
As memorable at a glance as marble but dying, reborn
Only another glance away, as the center
Of our attention, shifting at random
Everywhere like the sunlight,
Is caught by the play
Of light on all these surfaces, churnings and interweavings,
Upheavals, blossomings, an impulsive garden
Where we search and search as if for answers
And see its one reply:
Nothing is the same
Ever. This intricate bewilderment of currents,
In its least ripple, is unrepeatable.
The windbreak of alders we pass now,
The gravely leaning pale-boned
Row gone ashen,
Love, is another river, its bed channeled by seasons.
Our faces come near each other, mysterious
As water always. We cross a pool,
Translucent, the stones below us
Glimmering, remaining.

First Light

Before first light no sound
From the woods or the calm lake
Steel-gray in mist to its end
And even the creek's down-rush
On a stone bed gone still
As the owl that spoke for us
All night out of the hemlocks.

But now from the forest floor
(Dark green in a slow rain)
The voice of the winter wren—
Just as a touch of sun
Enlightens this good morning—
Begins its long cascading
Spillways and white rapids.

I see you wake, not moving
More than your eyelids
To listen, still half-held
By your dream, which was also mine
Between the owl and the wren:
That we'd learned how to fly
And sing by dark, by daylight.

You see my eyes have opened
With yours. Each of us turns
To the other, arms outstretched,
Then closed, both newly fledged
But as wing-sure at wakening
As owl-flight or wren-flight
And as song-struck as this dawn.

From *Walt Whitman Bathing* (1996)

ONE

The Pink Boy

The people had come to see
That boy in the living room
Of the house below our hill,
And my mother had brought me.

They had put him in a box
That was pink inside and out
On a table under a light
As pink as his pink suit.

He didn't look awake
Or asleep. He looked brand-new.
His mother said he'd had
Some milk from a bad cow.

He looked like something for sale
Downtown in a store window,
A doll or a parlor game.
I wanted to go home.

I said he was too pink.
I said he made me sick.
His mother said he'd been good,
Then turned her back and cried.

My mother said it was all
For the best if we only knew.
A man said he would fly
With a flock of angels now.

Another man said we could walk
Through the Valley of the Shadow
And never be afraid,
And then we had some cake.

The Laughing Boy

On my first day of school
My first friend was a boy
Who laughed at everything
We did on the playground.

He laughed on the high swings
And laughed on the teeter-totter
And laughed when he fell down
At the sound of the school bell.

His eyes squeezed shut. His cheeks
Crinkled against his nose.
His chin came jutting forward
And his mouth went *Haw haw haw.*

And I laughed too, but stopped
When we all marched up the stairs
And into the first grade
Of John Greenleaf Whittier

Grade School to learn how
To count and spell our names
And grow up and sing songs
And listen and sit still.

But my friend wouldn't behave.
He pointed at me and pointed
Around the room and stared
And laughed and sang to himself.

At noon, the teacher whispered
In his ear, gave him a note,
And said he should go now.
He cried. He cried like a baby,

And I walked home with him
Along the sandstone alley
To the tall gray broken house
Where his father read the message—

A quiet man, as short
As we were, with a mustache,
Suspenders, and four teeth—
Who told him to go to bed.

And that's what my friend did.
His father took a breath,
Nodded, shook my hand,
Smiled, and gave me an apple,

And as I crossed their yard,
My friend in a nightgown
Leaned out the attic window
And called my name and laughed.

Dizzy

I thought whirling
Back then I knew
Alone arms limp
In the yard spinning
Dizzy till both knees
Unbuckled our house
Tilting how to be
Happy go luckily over
Turning my head still
Wild my eyes through
Whirlpools of shingles down
A blurred muddle
Of leaves clouds all
Under gone toppling easy
In circling ripples
Slewed sideways
In a walleyed catty-
Cornered neighborhood too soon calmly
There again grass-flat plain Sunday-fixed
Tree trunks woodenly locked front doors
Upright no longer spun glassy like me like crazy.

My Father Laughing in the Chicago Theater

His heavy body would double itself forward
At the waist, swell, and come heaving around
To slam at his seatback, making the screws groan
And squawk down half the row as it went tilting
Under my mother and me, under whoever
Was out of luck on the other side of him.
Like a boxer slipping punches, he'd lift his elbows
To flail and jerk, and his wide-open mouth
Would boom out four deep *haaa*'s to the end of his breath.

He was laughing at Burns and Allen or Jack Benny
In person or at his limitless engagement
With Groucho, Chico, and Harpo. While my mother
Sat there between us, gazing at the stage
And chuckling placidly, I watched with amazement
The spectacle of a helpless father, unmanned,
Disarmed by laughter. The tears would dribble
From under his bifocals, as real as sweat.
He would gape and gag, go limp, and spring back to life.

I would laugh too, but partly at him, afraid
Of becoming him. He could scowl anywhere,
Be solemn or blank in church or going to work,
Turn grim with a cold chisel, or he could smile
At babies or football games, but he only laughed
There in that theater. And up the aisle
And through the lobby to the parking lot
And all the way home, I'd see the glow on his cheeks
Fade to the usual hectic steelmill sunburn.

By bedtime he was as somber as himself:
Two hundred and twenty horizontal pounds
Of defensive lineman, of open-hearth melter
Who could take the temperature of molten steel
At a glance, who never swore or told a joke.
Once, Jimmy Durante stopped, glared down at him,
And slapped his sides, getting an extra laugh
From my father's laugh, then stiff-leg-strutted away,
Tipping his old hat in gratitude.

My Passenger

I was flying solo in my father's car
For the first time. Man, I was on my way
From our rusty suburb to the heart of Chicago,
Full of the horsepower of his glory seat.

At the first stoplight inside the city limits,
A cop reached through the passenger-side window,
Opened the door and sprawled, grinning, beside me.
Where was I going? Fine. He needed a ride.

He slammed the door on his foot, then slammed it again
On the business end of his nightstick, then slammed it
Shut. I drove as if for a driver's test.
His huge red face stared at me, cold sober.

He was plastered. And I stiffened like a suspect
Sweating under the lights. Now he was slurring
His arch supports, the heat, and his uniform.
While passing the time of day, he passed out cold.

I had been booked for Amateur Afternoon
On the stage of the National Magic Company,
And my sportcoat bulged and rattled with delinquent
Treasures, all the gimmicks of my illusions:

Fake coins, cold decks, illegal homemade picklocks
I didn't know how to use except in daydreams
Of escaping like an artist, like a first
Offender out from under arrest, not guilty.

He spraddled there. His head lolled back. His mouth
Fell open, catching the breeze. His peaked cap tilted
Sideways across gray fringe and a bald spot.
The lipstick on his badge was the color of blood.

At every stop-and-go, the other drivers
Gaped at him, then at me. Officially injured
Or unofficially dead? Was I a snitch?
Was he my father? Were we practical jokes?

On the Outer Drive, his body slumped northeast,
And his cap flew off, back-flipping end over end.
In the rearview mirror, I saw it being run
Over and smashed flat and slapped to pieces.

So I kept going past the Field Museum
And bone-dry Buckingham Fountain (like my mouth)
And skimmed an island where the traffic cop
Was yelling at somebody else, not seeing us.

Then under the Elevated, he jerked awake,
Said *Here,* fumbled the door half open, squeezed
Himself outside while counting his handcuffs,
His wallet and gun-butt, stumbled, and went crawling

Up to the swaying curb. I drove away
Quickly and turned the corner. He was standing
Flatfooted like a man in a windy city,
Holding his ground and clutching his bare head.

That afternoon, I fooled almost everybody.

My Mother and Father

They stand by the empty car,
By the open driver's door,
Waiting. The evening sun
Is glowing like pig iron.

His red face hardens, goes flat
As if he's been told something
He doesn't want to hear
Or worry Mother about.

His faded denim work shirt
Hangs loose under his arms.
The holes burnt through the sleeves
Are ash-rimmed like his eyes.

She's wearing the new housecoat
That made her hands and feet
Disappear, and now her hair
Has tarnished like her silver.

As if ready to sing,
Her pale face trembling,
Softly, clearly, she says,
Where are we? We can't remember.

I say, *May I drive you somewhere?*
But they don't hear my voice.
We don't know who you are,
She says, and we stand there

Beside old tumbleweeds
Caught in a chain-link fence,
By the barbed wire and concrete
And slag in the rusty water.

Walking around the Block with a Three-Year-Old

She sees a starling legs-up in the gutter.
She finds an earthworm limp and pale in a puddle.
What's wrong with them? she says. I tell her they're dead.

She scowls at me. She stares at her short shadow
And makes it dance in the road. She shakes its head.
Daddy, you don't look pretty, she says. I agree.

She stomps on a sewer grid where the slow rain
Is vanishing. *Do you want to go down there?*
I tell her no. *Neither do I*, she says.

She picks up a stone. *This is an elephant.*
Because it's heavy, smooth, slate gray, and hers,
I tell her it's very like an elephant.

We're back. The starling is gone. *Where did it go?*
She says. I tell her I don't know, maybe
A cat took it away. *I think it's lost.*

I tell her I think so too. *But can't you find it?*
I tell her I don't think so. *Let's go look.*
I show her my empty hands, and she takes one.

A Woman Photographing Holsteins

Her slender body moves among the herd
On the grassy dike as surely as the sun
Goes down, as slowly
As they themselves can move one hoof at a time.

Their level spines are taller than she is,
Each flank a different country,
Islands of milk at nightfall, black-and-white
Deliberations of complete fulfillment.

She steps around the high gates of their thighs.
Their ears swivel,
And she takes in their deeply, broodingly
Contemplative profiles staring straight at her.

One bolts, but stops, having forgotten why.
The dewlap quivers. The veins
Of the udder pulse. As round, as large as her lens,
The eyes turn to the salt marsh and the sea.

She follows, kneels to focus, and with the gaze
Of the goddesses of meadows
The two of them wait there in the last of the light,
A horned moon rising. Then she rises too

And, smiling, comes my way, led by her shadow
Into my arms. We hum as if in clover.

At the Mouth of a Creek

This creek, as old as rain, flows past our fire
And, after a riffle and a broadening rush
On a spillway of gray-green stones, enters a river.
Evening without clouds under the hemlocks,
And the level sun is winnowing around us
In stems and stalks a thicket of gold light.
I've watched you stare at the incessantly
Changeable downheaval of a current
Ending as it began. Though it may alter
Quick moment by still moment like your eyes,
It stays translucent down to its wild bed.

Love, it was always you who brought me here,
Who came here with me, though I seemed alone,
Who stayed with me as the osprey turned above us
And we called the salmon home and the wren whispered
The almost silent song no one may hear
Without a change of mind, and it was you
Who burned with me that hour in the melting snow.
You had no name at first, no face, no voice,
But you became yourself in the real air
Beside me as our coupled imaginations,
Transfixed by the play of light, discovered us.

I've come to the creek's mouth and found you again.
Always before, my raw-edged restlessness
Took us away too soon. So let's lie down
And fill the night with our two shuddering hearts.
We have in us the same dust as these stones
Covered with golden algae and water moss
Like *dura mater*. The scattering of ashes
After our fire may bring us morning knowledge
At last to light our frail, permanent love.

TWO

Walt Whitman Bathing

After his stroke, he would walk into the woods
On sunny days and take off all his clothes
Slowly, one plain shoe
And one plain sock at a time, his good right hand
As gentle as a mother's, and bathe himself
In a pond while murmuring
And singing quietly, splashing a while
And dabbling at his ease, white hair and beard
Afloat and still streaming
Down his white chest when he came wading ashore
Naked and quivering. Then he would pace
In circles, sometimes dancing
A few light steps, his right leg leading the way
Unsteadily but considerately for the left
As if with an awkward partner.

He seemed as oblivious to passersby
As he was to his bare body, which was no longer
A nursery for metaphors
Or a banquet hall for figures of self-praise
But a bedroom or a modest bed in that bedroom
Or the covers on that bed
In need of airing out in the sunlight.
He would sit down on the bank and stare at the water
For an hour as if expecting
Something to emerge, some new reflection
In place of the old. Meanwhile, he would examine
The postures of wildflowers,

The workings of small leaves, holding them close
To his pale eyes while mumbling inaudibly.
He would dress then, helping
His left side with his right as patiently
As he might have dressed the wounded or the dead,
And would lead himself toward home like a dear companion.

The Rosebush

A memory of Theodore Roethke

He was going to plant a rose. He'd found it mildewed
In his garage where it had lain all spring
Still in its wrappings, putting out shoots
As pale as potato sprouts,
And now it was leaning in a bucket of water
To soak the sawdust off its roots for an hour.

A gift from a student, he said, a kind of homage.
He was planting it this late out of pure guilt.
He showed the label—*Peace*—and rumbled a slow
Half-strangled belly laugh,
Huddled over his rib cage, hunching broad shoulders
Under his sweatshirt, not quite spilling his drink.

Roses were too much trouble, too much pruning
And spraying and pampering. He hadn't planted
A single rosebush in his whole new garden.
You had to think about them
All year round and still give room and board
To aphids, leaf-rollers, earwigs, and black spot.

Besides, they'd been his father's meat, not his—
Otto, the greenhouse-keeper, King of the Roses,
Long-stemmed and fancy, big and tight as his fists.
Why should he grow flowers
Just for the cutting? Snip, and they were dead,
And you were a butcher, not a gardener.

He dug its hole with a spade, stooping and grunting
Angrily, impatiently, and jammed it
In, spreading the roots, bedding it down
With a hose and wads of compost
And slapping the mud smooth with his bare hands.
Then he leaned close, snarling, and kissed it twice.

And late that fall, in the middle of a party,
He took his drink outside and watered a bush
On which two roses, ragged, livid by moonlight,
Overblown and lopsided
Like the heads of broken puppets, were still dangling
From their thin stems. Grimly, he ate them both.

Love Still Has Something of the Sea

A few months before the outbreak of the Second World War,
I took a walk with Thomas Mann.
    —*Aldous Huxley,* Tomorrow and Tomorrow and Tomorrow

Aldous Huxley and Thomas Mann by the light
Gold after-light of a California sunset,
Strolled with their wives on a deserted beach
And spoke of Shakespeare, music, and Modern Love:
Was the Bitter Barren Woman of today
Even less knowable than the Fertile Goddess?

They mused there on the edge of America
Till their wives, who had drifted off, called their attention
To the outgoing tide and a phenomenon
In the sandy shallows: something like gray seaworms
Afloat or stranded, hundreds of thousands struggling
To mate or migrate beyond the Western world.

On closer look, they saw those quondam creatures,
Who made their way by means of the mass transport
Provided with a flush of embarrassment
By the City of the Angels and its outfall,
Were condoms joining the old tolerant sea.
They turned aside and talked about something else.

A Young Woman Trying on a Victorian Hat

She lifts it with both hands, murmurs the label,
And slowly crowns herself, amused, her mouth
A girl's mouth dreaming. There she is in the mirror,

Shifting to profile, one eye glancing under
Her lowered lashes, temporarily
Aloof from all these indiscreet attentions.

The bird of paradise feathers flirt at her ear.
She smiles beyond them, now enjoying the madness
Of a chance meeting after so many lovers.

Suddenly cool, she stares into a future
Where enormous doors swing wide for a dowager.
She firms her chin with a fervent sense of duty.

She lowers the veil and bows her head to flutter
Eye shadow at the burden of her grief.
Her lips go into mourning for loved ones.

Abruptly she takes it off and turns aside
To combs and purses, frowning seriously
And shaking her hair into a fresh disorder.

The Padded Cell

The only furniture is a man in a corner
Wearing his nakedness
As if he'd borrowed it from someone smaller.
He fidgets, it doesn't
Fit, he wants it off, he has nothing right
Or left to lose but his message
In this shut room and screams it silently
Through a secret passage
From his heart to his throat by the lectern of his tongue
Where he spills now
What he has to say for a soundless freedom of speech
And mouths it straight-
Forwardly up to a lightbulb shining down
On the blank canvas
Of the floor and walls, all padded to forgive
And forget those who trespass
Against them like this man who scrabbles erect,
Beginning to strut
And run away from it all through the looking glass
Of the Judas window
Before he comes to an abrupt conclusion
Smack up against it.

Blindman

He waits by the quiet street,
His cane, his fingers,
And his listening face
Trembling, not out of fear
But alert with wonder
At what lies just beyond
The end of what he is
And all he remembers
As now he steps forward
Into his near future
As deliberately as a spider
Scuttling from stone to curb
To stairway where he climbs
Into the spell of his room,
Where his light hands
Lead him to lie down,
Where slowly his mind's eye
Out of a different night
Lifts open like a moon.

THREE

Bear

You waken without moving. Your eyes are simply
Open now, your cheek and temple still
Against the cold flannel. The campfire
Has dwindled to amber.
Beyond its glow, a hulk, a darker blur
In the near darkness, huddled but seeming
Huge. The odor of pine tar
And rancid butter. Your mind says, *Bear.*

But not out loud. You've never felt more likely
To be quiet, to be motionless, to be
Thoughtful of others. Your instinct is to do
As little as possible: nothing,
Play dead. And then
At the very edge of hearing, a soft *huff.*
Even without touching, you know (the way
A blindman knows) something large is near you.

You try to ease the cramping in your calves
While your feet consider lurching you upright
And running away with you. But you remember,
Out of all those missing hikers and sleepers,
The few returning (maimed, in tatters)
Advised against such short-term leaps of faith
In their disjointed memoirs,
So you lie rigid, hoping you're only dreaming.

You've dreamed of bears,
But the sweat of your brow and the slipknot
In your solar plexus
Are matters of raw fact. Though you've been haunted
Before by monsters of your own invention
By daylight while you lay
Stark, staring awake, here something
Real, you realize, is really brushing your foot.

Again, you lift one eyelid. The fire coals have dimmed
To auburn, and you see the heavy shape
Between you and the light, not sly, not cautious
But naturally, easily silent as it moves
By the corner of your eye to the other darkness
Where nothing now but a moth touches the night.
You wait what seems an hour, blinking, then quiver
To sleep, still making no one of yourself.

A Pair of Barn Owls, Hunting

Now slowly, smoothly flying over the field
Beside the orchard into the after-light
Of the cold evening, the ash gold owls come sailing
Close to the branches, gliding across the arbor
Where the bare grapevines ripen only shadows
In the dead of winter, and at the end of a garden
Suddenly flare their wings, hover,
And swerve, claws first, down to the grass together.

For a Woman Who Phoned *Poetry Northwest* Thinking It Was *Poultry Northwest*

How can you give your chickens a quick molt?
Madam, no earthly and no heavenly knowledge
Is alien to poets or their organs
Of inspiration. Feed your whole flock lightly
For two full weeks. They'll lose weight and forget
To lay more eggs. Next, feed them heavily
On rations lavishly rich in nitrogen.
They'll molt then, and their new plumage will be
Beautifully close-bedded against winter.

Think of us out in the cold in our old feathers
As you scatter grain. We are sincerely yours.

Living with Snakes

Since their natural habitat with its wide secret
Night-long itinerary
Is impossible for you to reproduce,
Your snakes will be
Unhappy living with you. Though you give them
Their stones and water,
Sand, ultraviolet light, and hiding places,
Serve embryo mice
And daily (gently, gingerly) touch and soothe
Their one-way scales,
They will scarcely look at you without recoiling.
Though you make a nest
In the branches of your stiffened hands and fingers,
They will climb beyond it,
Searching for more than you at the end of you.
What is it they want?
Not simply to shed their skins or to escape
From their pet master,
But to become what doesn't exist, to remain
At length inside their bodies
Yet to reach a place where they have none at all.
Though you may offer
The run of the house to them, from basement to attic,
The hollows of your walls,
The luxurious pillows of your insulation,
They will reappear
Dissatisfied some pale morning, having been trailed
Through those headlong retreats
By their followers, by processions of rib cages,
By their narrowest selves.

Clancy the Burro's First Day in Heaven

He wakens on bright straw.
Through his open-ended stall
He can see the gates to the meadow
And the orchard are swung wide,
And he goes through both and drinks
From the washtub and the creek
And dines on blackberry leaves,
The tips of hazel branches,
Sugar, and windfall apples.

At noon, there are no flies,
No halters, and no horses.
At two o'clock, no strangers
With funnels and syringes.
At four, no clumsy riders,
No hobbles or crosstrees.
At six, there are no dogs.

At sundown he hears his name
Being called from far away,
And he trots toward that sound
On small precise hooves
That can take their places
Carefully among stones
On the narrowest of paths.
His breath comes huffing the first
Deep-seated note of his call
But stops there when he stops
And shies and stands still
Just out of reach of the hands
Offering rolled oats.

He stretches his neck slowly
Till his loose, trembling lips
Can touch the finger-ends
And his breath half scatters, half catches
The prize, and he munches
Aloud with perfect grinders
As humbly, as seriously
As a daily communicant.

The currycomb moves across
The high crest of his rump
And the base of his switching tail.
His coat gleams, blue and silver.
The upright human bodies
Nearby now hold their ground
Firmly while he leans
Against them, against them,
Their fingers rubbing the deep
Soft ermine of his ears.

The hands and the bodies go.
He watches from the shade,
And braying his only song
From tenor to alto,
From bass to boy soprano
Again and again, he turns
To browse the heavenly night.

For the Young Vine Maples

If they sprout deep in thickets,
Their branches grope
Upward crookedly left or down
And right among tanglefooted elders,
Their leaves stretched out
Through salal, through hazel
For the least light-hold.

If they find no sky halfway
Their own, they stay
Alive where they are, the green boughs
Dipping to root again and again, almost
Unbreakably supple
Under the treads and blades
Of loggers and earth-movers.

But even cut half through, bent
Backward, left for dead, fire-checked
With slash or buried
Crushed in snag-filled ditches,
They will break out by spring
In shadows, searching once more
For light they may never find.

If moved into a garden then, they rise
Slowly and slowly straighten
To a grove of slender trees,
The first to go blood-red and amber
By the end of summer, lingering
Long into every winter
For one death after another.

For a Young Shield Fern

It needs almost no light. It grows
    On the forest floor
Under the sweep and windfall
    Of firs and alders,
Under dead branches softened
    Long through their seasons
Mingled with leaves fading
    Web-thin,
Shrunken, its first unfolding
    Inch-long fronds like feathers
Of green frost, its roots
    Shallow. Why
Should the small veins deepen
    Or spread wide
Ever? Rain and the remnants
    Of rain and dewfall
And the rising mist have left
    No interval
As they meet and linger, snowfall, even
    Slower snow-melt
Together all winter. My fingers
    Reenter the earth
Beneath it almost as easily
    As water and lift it
Gently, trembling in my palm,
    Itself in the light
Handful of death from which it opened
    Again. It goes
With me out of the forest
    Into the garden.

SEQUENCE: LANDSCAPES

Mapmaking

It's an old desire: a sketch of part of the earth
There in your hands. You touch it, saying, *There.*
So make your map:
If you have no crossroads, no confluence of streams
To set your starting point, you simply pretend
You know where you are
And begin outlining a landscape, using a compass
And your measured stride toward landmarks: thrusts of bedrock,
Trees or boulders, whatever
Seems likely to be around after you've gone.
You fix your eyes on them, one at a time,
And learn the hard way
How hard it is to fabricate broken country.
You go where your line takes you: uphill or down,
Over or straight through,
Between and past the casual, accidental
Substance of this world. Once there, you turn back
To confirm your bearings,
To reconcile what you saw with what you see,
Comparing foresight and hindsight. These are moments
When your opinion
Of yourself as cartographer may suffer.
Your traverse *ought* to return to its beginning,
To a known point, though you,
Slipshod, footsore by dusk, may find your hope
Falls short of perfection: remember no one
Really depends on you
To do away with uncertainty forever.
Your piece of paper may seem in years to come
An amusing footnote

For wandering minds, a record of out-of-the-way
Transfixions (better preserved by photographers)
Whose terrain is so far askew
It should be left to divert imaginations
Like yours that enjoy believing they've mapped out
Some share of the unknown.

On a Mountainside

Here on the north face, on a slab of granite
With a fractured overhang like a lean-to,
You take your time
To look at the horn peaks and truncated spurs
Of another ridge whose three cirques tilt their glaciers
As if to pour them
Over their brims and down to a hanging valley.
You stare that way and try hard to remember
How you once thought
But instead sit down astonished, stunned, astounded—
Your words all formed from *stone* and turning to stone
Again like your lips and tongue
While you catch your breath as slowly and painlessly
As you can. The ropes and hardware at your feet
Seem faintly familiar.
The blue-white hand in front of your face has been there
Before if you're not mistaken. This halfway house
Is cold enough
To impress the least impressionable person
You know, who at the moment seems to be you.

The temptation here, the rapture of these heights,
Is supposed to be Wagnerian grandeur,
Getting above yourself
And looking down on too much of the world,
Confusing elevation with mastery,
Playing King of the Hill.
But you don't feel like that. You had no chance
To name this much-climbed mountain and no flag
To plant, gnomic *or* tribal.
And you didn't get to the top. You scrambled for less
Out of a lack of skill, from fatigue, from fear
Of missing a handhold.
What have you gathered now but blisters and windburn,
Calluses and a fondness for oxygen?

That your inclination here is to hold still,
To make no random moves, no idle gestures.
That your whole body
Has turned as dangerous and indelicate
As high explosives. That this chunk of ice,
Solid, perdurable
As a rock and far less likely to dissolve
Than you, is the pure embodiment of the desire
To fall. That if you drop it
Now, it will fall as far as you can tell
All the way to the ocean without pausing
To be True or Beautiful.
That it formed a poor impression of your hands.
That the earth is much more stony than motherly.
That the closer you come
To any mountain, the harder it is to see.
That lightheadedness is not illumination.

That the odds are no one ever before has lingered
Exactly where you're sitting and seen exactly
Everything you take in
From your eccentric viewpoint. Isn't that something?
Presuming you'll be able to stand up
And climb back down
To the place you came from, what remains? Some scratches
You leave behind to melt in the first thaw.
But didn't you have the guts
To admit you'd reached the point of no return?
Isn't *that*, at least, a kind of evening knowledge,
Like it or not?
At nearly the same angle as all three snow fields
The late afternoon sun comes rushing and skimming
Toward you, through your eyes,
And through your trembling, stiffening fingers
In a dazzle of light, a burnt-gold avalanche.

By a Waterfall

Over the sheer stone cliff-face, over springs and star clusters
Of maidenhair giving in and in to the spray
Through thorn-clawed crookshanks
And gnarled root ends like vines where the sun has never from dawn
To noon or dusk come spilling its cascades,
The stream is falling, at the brink
Blue-green but whitening and churning to pale rain
And falling farther, neither as rain nor mist
But both now, pouring
And changing as it must, exchanging all for all over all
Around and past your shape to a dark-green pool
Below, where it tumbles
Over another verge to become a stream once more
Downstream in curving slopes under a constant
Cloud of what it was
And will be, and beside it, sharing the storm of its arrival,
Your voice and all your words are disappearing
Into this water falling.

On the Plains

There was nothing to keep you here, and there was nothing
To keep you from returning, so now you stand
In this plain country where a river stone
Seems lost, a tree impractical, where walking
Measures your time and space as plodding equals,
Where even a change of weather has no point
Of ambush, no hiding place but the horizon.

You see what there is to see as far away
As a buzzard in this Land of Hope Deferred:
Whatever is going to happen—relief or ruin,
Rescue or massacre—is obvious
So long ahead of time, you can relax
And, meanwhile, make yourself uncomfortable,
Acquiring a taste for painless disappointment.

To live here is to take the Middle of Nowhere
To heart against plain speech and desolation,
And growing means to keep the Eternal Now
Coldly in mind, a potato in a cellar,
Eyes clenched to hold the past and future tight,
And dying is no harder than busting sod
Or breaking new ground on the flats of righteousness.

While barbed wire cuts the grids of your neighborhood
Into lots, boneyards, and pens, while the walls of houses
Measure you foursquare, while shaded windows
And roofs keep out the mad lights in the sky,
The medicines of choice are dancing and shouting:
Stomping your bootsoles on a floor and saving
The jam-packed firmament from election to Hell.

If you go away again, not breaking the Laws
Of Diminishing Returns or False Perspective
Or Parsimony, nothing will interfere
Except the sun and snow and rain and a god
Who takes the shape of the prevailing wind:
A mass as heavy as the fear of the known,
Which, though you cringe aside, still moves against you.

In a Pasture

Past outcrops of gray stone on a sloping field,
By heather and buttercups, a flock of sheep
Is grazing under the sun, black faces bowed.
Beyond them, the strewn clouds
Are almost motionless, the shades of driftwood
In a sky bright to the blue edge of trembling.

But over the pond beside you, the mayflies
Dance with an air grown cool
To their touch. A meadowlark
Half mutes its call, divided and plaintive
Now like the splintered pipes of Pan
Announcing an end to all your pastorals.

You're lying here
In the sure and certain hope of remembering
No matters of fact. You want to believe
Someone like you could lie down in green pastures
And restore his soul,
That sheep might safely graze, that the earth itself
Could turn magnanimous, could suffer its children
To live on nothing but pleasant surfaces.

Now you remember buttercups are poison
And somebody has to dip the lambs for lice,
Dock all their tails, treat them for stomach worms
And nasal gleet, castrate the bucks, and fleece
The elders till some tame bellwether
Leads the survivors to the butcher shop.

A sheepdog, crouching, circling, gathers the flock
Swiftly, outfacing rams, outbluffing yearlings,
And then stops cold
To study what you are. After a moment
He remembers. He takes your measure
With a growl, dismisses you, and herds them away,
Panting, ecstatic, toward his whistling master.

By a River

Your choice was always clear: not the long struggle
Upstream against the current, against the constant
Headlong pummeling of snow-melt and downpour
Nor the leaf-slow easy drifting
Downstream, the way all trees on a cutbank bend
Before they fall, but simply staying
Here by the river where you watch and wait
For what appears, moves past, and vanishes.

You've learned what you can about this watery sky,
Its rearrangement of your slight reflections,
Its turmoil, each moment so subtly various,
You can hardly tell, can hardly remember
What you marveled over only a glance before:
The shimmering, the lovely formalities
Of a chaos you can touch with your finger-ends,
A surface whose tarnished and burnished galaxies
Are born and borne away, but instantly
Return in a translucent blossoming.

You know under that surface always, no matter
What may seem apparent by sunlight,
Cloudlight, or moonlight, another life is passing,
Not just the stones and snags, the common bed-load
Of all rivers, not only the star-backed swimmers
Whose falls and springs once dazzled you into believing
You could dream your way to the source, but the Other

Whose body is never still, is always turning
Away from you downriver as if to stream
To an end beyond you through the deepest channels,
And yet remains beside you, whose light is lighter
Than air, whose breath is water, whose water is light.

On the Forest Floor

In this green shade, over the leaves and rubble
Of the fallen and still falling, over branches
And tangles of tree roots, over whole stones
And whole nurse logs, beneath the arches
Of ferns and the grottoes of deadfalls,
The moss has spread and deepened an underworld.

You kneel here naturally, and the air around you
Yields to your touch like moss, as the moss itself
Will yield to snow and ice through winter
To return as what it was,
And the green air you breathe is yielding to rain
Softer than moss, suspended like a cloud.

And moss—the only living substance here
For which a speck of sky after the death
Of a leaf is not an oracular emptiness—
The cold before the cold—
Has no need to fall. It was born fallen
And can live in its own light, by its own light.

The closer you look at it, the more it changes
To the landscapes of the earth,
The yet-to-be and the dead and the newly risen
Merged into rootless lives whose entrances,
Like your lost eyes, become what enters them,
Where all that endures is your bewilderment.

In a Field of Wildflowers

Above the river, over the broad hillside
And down the slope in clusters and strewn throngs,
Cross-tangled and intermingled,
Wildflowers are blooming, seemingly all at once
And all together, the purple, crimson, and white
Of lupine and larkspur,
Paintbrush and everlasting, a lavish outbreak
That, seen far off, is merely spectacular
But here, up close,
As luminous as the dawn of the first day
Or a dream of the burgeoning of galaxies.

Today a beeline is a drunken spiral
From flower to flower, a quizzing of yellow jackets,
And a looping sideslip
Over a scurry of ants going up or down
The stems that bear their nectar in hanging gardens.
With a metallic whir
A rufous hummingbird in a blurred streak
Swoops out of somewhere to a flowerhead,
Hums, hovers—
An amber-and-brass hook suspended from nothing—
Then vanishes, cackling, into quickened air.

And we stand still, up to our knees in summer.
We have a sense of being here in disguise,
Under false pretenses,
Of suffering from an embarrassment of the riches
Of others, of being shut out: the only members
Of the three kingdoms
We can see or hear or name who don't belong,
Whose every step is a natural disaster,
Who have no cause
For trespassing but envy and a desire
For the eyes of bees in faceted starbursts.

This is a field where lovers have run barefoot,
Carefree and laughing, into each other's arms
In ads and commercials.
But on clay like miniature badlands and broken shale
And the tough, embedded patches of weeds fighting
For root-room and sunlight,
Lovers would trip and fall, crumpled in pain,
Unable to touch, their hearts and soles in ribbons.
So what's left here for us
In this short season before the petals wither
And the snow returns, deeper than all these blossoms,

And the birds and bees are off on another round
And the ants go back to the business of the earth?
Should we sing or dance?
Or have our less-than-ambrosial repast
Cross-legged and brooding? Drink ourselves somber?
Or quietly presume
Out of honest destitution to share the wealth
Of emissaries with roots and nests and wings
Without their consent
For as long as we can imagine through a clear
Benevolent afternoon that has no end?

New Poems

The Silence of the Stars

When Laurens van der Post one night
    In the Kalihari Desert told the Bushmen
        He couldn't hear the stars
Singing, they didn't believe him. They looked at him,
    Half-smiling. They examined his face
        To see whether he was joking
Or deceiving them. Then two of those small men
    Who plant nothing, who have almost
        Nothing to hunt, who live
On almost nothing and with no one
    But themselves, led him away
        From the crackling thorn-scrub fire
And stood with him under the night sky
    And listened. One of them whispered,
        Do you not hear them now?
And van der Post listened, not wanting
    To disbelieve, but had to answer,
        No. They walked him slowly
Like a sick man to the small dim
    Circle of firelight and told him
        They were terribly sorry,
And he felt even sorrier
    For himself and blamed his ancestors
        For their strange loss of hearing,
Which was his loss now. On some clear nights
    When nearby houses have turned off their visions,
        When the traffic dwindles, when through streets
Are between sirens and the jets overhead
    Are between crossings, when the wind
        Is hanging fire in the fir trees,
And the long-eared owl in the neighboring grove
    Between calls is regarding his own darkness,
        I look at the stars again as I first did
To school myself in the names of constellations
    And remember my first sense of their terrible distance,
        I can still hear what I thought

At the edge of silence were the inside jokes
        Of my heartbeat, my arterial traffic,
                The C above high C of my inner ear, myself
Tunelessly humming, but now I know what they are:
        My fair share of the music of the spheres
                And clusters of ripening stars,
Of the songs from the throats of the old gods
        Still tending even tone-deaf creatures
                Through their exiles in the desert.

In the House of the Dragon

It comes through the open door as if it's late
For a celebration, a dragonfly, brilliant green,
Three inches long but seeming a yard wide,
A blur jamming three hundred million years
Into itself sideways, over and out
Of the hall to dart through the living room, all done
To a turn in the dining room to levitate,
To rearrange directions, focused beyond
Me staring hard behind the times where it *was*,
With my hands and portable feet to wish it well
Or ill or somewhere else before it's there
Now, hanging fire near a window, not hammerheading
The glass like a hornet but immediately
In the bathroom mirror brushing itself aside
To shower, humming in less than a split second
From curtains on the verge of plumbing, the heights
And depths of porcelain, gone to frisk the terrain
Of obstacles in a bedroom, to reconnoiter
Cover and field of fire, to counter-retreat
In future engagements, suddenly riveted,
Perched, a horizontal spur on the finial
Of a desk lamp, scanning all multimedia
With a globular goggling pair of sepia eyes
That meet at the top of its head where still another
Black-and-white target eyespot dreams whatever
Its other thousands haven't, its emerald
Thorax glittering, its ovipositor
On the level, shut, straight out, in neutral, its turquoise
Abdomen pulsing when I approach,
Yawing away, its body hung from the sheen
Of four transparent winglets, carried off
To dangle helpless under its own power
With a lifetime pass through any and every
Open doorway simultaneously
In every room with a right of every passage
To skim all surfaces everywhere without fear,

Yet just as suddenly absent, gone, no longer
Anywhere to be found, though slowly I tour
And prowl each room for it, make room, stand by
The door to look, to listen, to search again
And finally sit silent in what should seem
My own house mostly paid for but unsettling
Down now, useless, barren of good works,
Weary, stale, unprofitably flattened
Without its bearer of inscrutable good
Bad news, its going concern with schemes ablaze,
Its mind intent on all the unknowable
Guesswork of mere mammals dispossessed
At a loss for its passion to this very day.

Recital

During your song, the audience shouldn't know
    You have any longing to breathe
        The same air they do. The art of singing
Is first of all to conceal the art
    Of breathing. Midway in some rare
        Breathtakingly passionate expenditure
From your lungs and throat, they should never guess
    Your mind is dying to reach the end of that passage
        Where once more you may inhale
What you've been pouring out for them
    In strains of music. You must seem completely
        At your ease, in no way
Nearly exhausted while you try to express
    Some inexpressibly heartfelt
        Sustained feeling promised once
In sweat and hope by your composer
    And now by you. You do not gasp
        Or show under your makeup the crow's-feet
And creasing of heavy labor or suffer
    The first quaint symptoms of asphyxiation,
        And when the last note
Disappears from between your lips,
    You hold yourself as still
        As if you were drawn from nature. You wait
As the final chords go on without you, acknowledging
    No applause till the accompaniment
        Has closed its own mouth and eyelids. Even then,
Though you smile and allow yourself
    To seem half-pleased, to be
        Touched, to be slightly inclined
Forward at neck and waist, to recognize flowers
    At your feet, and a few faces,
        You show no sign of breathing.

Recitation

He had to say a poem. Others before him
Got up and said their poems. Some of them
Remembered everything they were supposed to,
And some of them cried when they couldn't get the words
Right with their lips as stiff as Popsicles.

One of them didn't say anything, just stood there
And stared at his mother on the edge of her pew
Nodding and staring back, and one nice girl
Told about flowers and looked like one and smiled,
Making her hands go up and down like petals

And butterflies, and everyone murmured
And whispered how nice she was. Then his own mother
Led him by the hand up the three steps
And let him go by himself on the flat part
To the middle place where he was supposed to turn

And face the people. He was supposed to say
The poem he'd been told in his left ear
At bedtime for a week. It said he was sitting
Down on a bumpy log, being as grumpy
As he could be, while a little bullfrog

Called from a bog, *Cheer up! Cheer up!* and sounded
So funny, the boy in the poem had to laugh.
And *he* was supposed to laugh, but he wouldn't do it.
He'd seen a frog and a bog, had sat on a log,
But frogs didn't sound funny, and though he remembered

Everything he was supposed to say to these people,
He didn't want to say it. His mother was looking
Sad and his father inside his Sunday suit
Was turning red, and just when they all thought
He wasn't going to say it, he said it

Loudly in a slow sarcastic singsong,
And they never asked him to recite another.

A Letter Home

In a bad year, my father went away
A hundred miles to take the only job
He could find. Two nights a week he would sit down
In his boardinghouse after a hard shift
In the open hearth and write a duty letter.
He hated telephones, being hard of hearing
And hard of speaking and just as hard of spending
Now that he had to save our car and our house
And feed us from long distance. He knew words
Of all kinds, knew them cold in Latin
And Greek, from crossword puzzles and cryptograms,
But hardly any of them would come from his mouth
Or find their way onto paper. He wrote my mother
Short plain sentences about the weather
And, folded inside each single page, for me,
In colored pencils, a tracing of a cartoon
From the funny papers: Popeye or Barney Google
Or Mutt and Jeff or the Katzenjammer Kids.
The voice-balloons hanging over their heads
Said, "Hope to see you soon" or "Hello, David."
And those would be his words for months on end.

I thank him now for his labor, his devotion
To duty, and his doggedness. I was five,
And he was thirty-five. I have two daughters
As young as I was then (though I'm twice as old
As my father was). If I had to leave them
In a bad year, I'd want them to be good
To their mother and to love her as much as I did.
I'd miss them, and I'd want them to be happy
With or without me and to remember me.
If I could manage, I'd even write them love
In a letter home with traces of me inside.

A Summer Storm in Navarre, Ohio

When the wind was right, all of my grandma's house
Smelled like the girl in the bakery next door
Who worked by the fan-vent. We were both sixteen.
She had dark eyes and a creamy country look,

And her uniform was smoother than meringue.
When I bought our daily bread, she showed me around
An oven brooding cupcakes like young chicks
And a dipstick swirling batter. I made a date.

That night I lay in my great-grandpa's bed
In the attic room, not praying myself to sleep
Like an old United Brethren circuit-rider,
But falling down and around in a storm of dreams,

All featuring Mary Haas whose body language
Had spoken volumes to me. She looked so wholesome,
So filled with natural ingredients,
I wanted to add the butter and plum jam.

I drove her in my grandma's '40 Nash
At the wartime limit—35 miles per hour—
Eight miles through farmland to the nearest movie
With my learner's permit, speaking when spoken to

But trying to be a farm girl's city boy
Who didn't go to church, who recited Browning,
Who'd been in a school play, who could hum Tchaikovsky,
Who shaved each week, who'd almost felt up a girl.

She had dressed fragrantly in a flowery dress
As stiff as a chintz curtain, and though her knees
And thighs were somewhere under there when she sat,
They stayed in place, uncrossed, firmly together.

Yet we held hands. No doubt a movie unreeled,
But its name, nature, and plot made no impression.
We were the stars. I remember only our fingers
Quivering, parting, touching again, perspiring.

I drove us home in the gusty wind and rain,
And while I imagined kisses or daring clutches
Here or there or thereafter, a state policeman
Arrested our progress on that country road

And told us to drive on, even more slowly,
To stay in our car in case another tornado
Followed the first. We crept. For two straight miles
The telephone poles, uprooted and strewn aside,

Sprawled in the dark cornfields, plucked and twisted,
Thrown up and around and down just minutes before.
We counted them, but lost count while they drove
Us and the storm home like a moral lesson.

We said good night. I kissed her lamely, shaken
By guilt as if by Grandma. Her lipstick trembled
Against my ordinary lips for the first time
And the last. I climbed the stairs and sank into bed

Saying good-bye, good luck to the underworld
Of her underwear, as bottomless as the powers
Of the night in the cornfields where the telephone poles
Were lying still and sleeping it off, no more

Messages on those wires for a while for the in-
Terrupted lovers of Stark County, Ohio,
For the best-worst days of a summer so long ago,
I hardly remember just how terrible

It was to lie awake where my great-grandpa
Had slept more reverently than I wanted to
And died and stiffened alone. Then came the dawn
And the smell of fresh bread whirling through the window.

The Young Goats

For Nimrod and Rameses

The theory was they'd eat the blackberry patch
    That clogged a third of my two acres
        With impenetrable archways. Oh, all goats
Love those leaves, people said. They'd strip the vines
    Better than machines. I bought two knee-high weanlings,
        A Swiss patched black and white with pricked ears
And the look of a child just this moment invited
    To be the big surprise at a party
        And a buff Nubian with drooping ears
And a permanent half-smile. Their house
    Was a chicken coop inherited as is
        From the previous lord of my land
With the upper crust of fossilized chicken droppings
    Still intact. They took one tour
        And then slept under it. They nibbled
A few of the youngest and most tender
    Blackberry leaves, blinking, staring at nothing,
        Rotating their underjaws and salivating
Like connoisseurs, and then went back
    To pellets. What they wanted
        Was to skip, jump, clamber, and climb
On anything that was taller than they were,
    The pinnacle of delight being my car
        Where they would sharpen their hoofs
And then stand braced foursquare
    For the unfolding of events on the highway.
        But most of all they wanted to be *near* me,
To plant two cloven feet, even
    Three or four in my lap whenever I had one,
        And then with their victim's eyes,
Through horizontal pupils designed to scan
    The whole horizon for predators
(Whose slitted upright pupils fed
    A narrower purpose), they would gaze
        Through my ambiguously circular holes

In search of some lost paradise. One time,
      Before I gave them shamefaced to a farmer,
            They ran with me through the knee-high grass
(My pipes of Pan two bottles of cold beer),
      And together we stomped down a playing field
            The size of a picnic table, doing stiff-legged
Swivels, pogo-sticking, and when I flopped,
      Exhausted, they leaned over my face and stared
            Sincerely deep through my eyes
At the landscape floating in the back of my mind
      And bleated softly, calling for the others,
            For the good goats no longer grazing there.

In a Garden

The day you said you loved me, we found ourselves
    In a public garden, and we sat together
        On a cold stone bench, holding each other's hands
As if we were making certain
    They were our own hands. I tried to tell you
        I had loved you too, but from so far away
Through so much hesitation, so much restraint
    And disbelief across our strict profession
        Of words, our unwritten law (the years,
The years), I couldn't say your name to myself
    By daylight or think of you
        As more than a faint hope from a different life
Now left and lost. In our garden
    All that changed: everything spoke
        Of surrender and rearrangement, of intermingling
In a pattern bedded by landscape gardeners
    Who had crossed a shelter with a carnival
        And a nursery at the growing ends of the earth
To blossom all year round. Each touch
    (Even your shoulder against mine) was a fire
        Between us of such impulsive splendor,
I felt I'd become a time-lapse visual aid
    For botanists, my body ready
        To burst and bloom and scatter a nebula
Out of the multilayered sheaths
    Of an old husk, to spread its wealth
        Beyond what recently had been a mind
But now was a zodiac of perennials
    Dreamed of by Andrew Marvell
        At the center of his paradise. Both of us
Accepted the rules of gardens: Here you may grow
    Safely to be admired for your own sake,
        To be cared for only as well
As you've been caring, and here you may flourish
    Briefly and go to seed in isolation,
        Deceptively beautiful

In the eyes of butterflies and a half-blind world
That can only guess what you've become
In each other's eyes. We knew
We would have to go on our still separate ways
That very evening though we lingered, pretending
We were the first to name whatever we saw:
The moss and ferns, the birds, the fruit of the trees,
The absent serpent (whose temptation
Would have been welcome), the angel
Asleep at the gate (having grown tired of waiting),
And the invertebrate sluggish god of our fathers
(Looking the other way).

Alexandra and the Spiders

Because she wanted the girl next door as a friend,
Five-year-old Alexandra helped her mother
Make spiders out of crackers and peanut butter
With pretzel-stick legs and bulging raisin eyes.

And her father helped her carry a plate of them
To the strange porch and helped her ring the doorbell
And helped her spill them on the welcome mat
At the feet of the other mother and her daughter.

While her father helped Alexandra gather spiders
Stuck together wrong side up, sweet eyes
Sunk, their legs out of order, the kindly neighbor
Invited Alexandra to step inside.

But she, feeling helpless, clumsy, and hopeless
Like her father, shook her head no, shying away
Though the other mother smiled and offered her hand
And bit a spider in half with her front teeth.

Her father took her home where, in the kitchen,
Alexandra broke into tears, explaining between
Sobs she couldn't untie her tongue to say
Or do what she most wanted to: her brain

Had been shaking back and forth, she said, and she shook
Her body back and forth like a prisoner
Tied in a cage. She squirmed, all legs and eyes,
Then sank to her knees and hid her face in her hands.

Her mother and father with their arms around her
Tried to make her feel what she ought to feel,
But she felt only herself caught by herself
For the first time, held fast in the wrong place.

In the Shadow

The moon has come between us
And the sun. It hovers now
Exactly over that face,
Casting a cone of shadow
Around us in the garden.

And suddenly it's evening,
A brief twilight without
The reckoning of nightfall,
A shade within which all
Certainty turns to chance.

Sparrows and crows are falling
Still in the branches. A moth
Alights at a trumpet's mouth,
And my hand once more discovers
Yours, recovers yours.

We stand in the earthshine,
Remembering night comes
And goes, that we give ourselves
The coincidence of arriving
Just in time to be gone,

That night and day are nothing
But interruptions of light,
That its capture and release
Are fully as much as lives
Are worth in the short run.

This shortest of nights
Is ours to fill, not with stars
But the bright particulars
Of ourselves, till we find again
As at love's beginning

For a moment our awkward age,
The presumption of innocence
And all of our lost labors,
Where the curvatures of the moon
And the earth and our light bodies

Will prove one and the same,
Where the crooked is made round
And the stony soft, and the gray
Glistens a while, and daylight
Turns us a blind eye.

Looking for Shiva in the Public Market

Only one place in the entire city
Has Shiva for sale—on a low-down dark half-level,
A shop the size of a toll booth wedged between
Gaggles of aging knickknacks, tricks, and the latest
Reproductions of primitive artifacts.
Mr. Mukerjee has promised to be open
To me this workday morning, but he is closed.

Through two small cluttered windows, I can see
Nothing beyond the brassware even resembling
The circle of flares and the leaping hair of the dancer
I dreamed of buying for the impending birthday
Of the woman I love. Perhaps Mr. Mukerjee
Has no Shiva but, being agreeable
With my anxious voice on the phone, was afraid to say so.

To kill some time, I browse through copies of charms,
Mass-produced fetishes and nightmare-catchers,
Among the paraphernalia of decommissioned
Officers of ex-armies and ex-navies,
The gimmicks of disillusioned conjurors,
And the sheepskinned bleating of diploma mills:
Trinkets of old orders, guesswork, and fears.

My wife, who is wiser and more intelligent
And far more knowledgeable than I am, tells me
Shiva renewed her life. She wants him near.
But I must teach now. The meter is turning red
By my parked car, and it's a ten-minute walk
To plug it and ten more back. I'm running out
Of time, and here and now is my last chance.

Behold and lo! It's Mr. Mukerjee
Manifesting himself in beard and turban.
He produces Shiva from the unmanifest
Transcendence of a box. I strike a bargain
With a plastic amulet and carry off
Under my arm, not burdens of circumstance
And error, but a copper and silver god.

My right hand feels the drumbeat of our pulse.
My left hand holds the phenomenal world aflame.
My second right hand lifts to say, *Fear not.*
My other left hand points to my left foot
Rising to stomp its way through any jungle.
My right foot treads the demon of Oblivion,

And my head is balanced now, serene and still
At the center of creation and destruction.
My hair is afloat with fire. I drink the morning
On this northern shore, beside the trafficking,
Raggedly rummaging, burgeoning, grotesquely
Changeable, spontaneous, temporarily
Eternal sea, to rise beyond mere selfhood.

Shiva, when drunk, would dance home to his wife.

The Return of Orpheus

On the long way up from Hell, he listened hard
To the footsteps of Eurydice behind him
At first, making sure (though forbidden to look back)
She was still there. But he couldn't keep from thinking
How well he'd played for Hades and his queen
In spite of the sulphurous air and the foul acoustics.

Since the rock stairs were smooth, he strummed a little,
Recalling one clear strain of improvisations
He'd used for the Underworld: it was so bizarre—
And despite the pressure!—why, for the gods' sake,
Hadn't he been gambling for his love?
Most would have played it safe with memorized themes
And old variations, but he'd taken chances,
Had proved himself again among melting stones
And the shades of shade trees, making that black rubble,
Those half-charred simulacra, pull themselves
Together and shuffle by like immortal souls.

For Eurydice, he'd given the performance
Of his life, had almost given his all for her
Sweet eyes and ears, for the incomparable body
Of her womanly wisdom. She was his accomplice,
His accompaniment, his countervailing confluence,
Who could tell him, always, which was the finer nuance
And the right embellishment, which ornamentation
For codettas mezzo forte was most telling.

She was a nonesuch, a nonpareil, yet seemed
Pallid and slightly wilted now, a flower
Long after the rainy season. Had there been
No music for her in Hell to lift her heart
To her throat in his absence but wild shrieks and groans?

But that would end. Now he would play for her
(Without looking back) to raise her fallen spirits:
A medley of her favorites, even some new ones
Composed in her absence, despite it, because of it.
She with her natural instinct for the best,
Her sure sense of direction in the myriad
Pathways of melody, would again take heart
As his lute plucked out: *This is the way to the world.*
We'll find once more the love we knew before death.

And he played more beautifully and suddenly
More strangely and compellingly than ever
And more hauntingly: his fingers no longer
His own but quickly becoming more like muses
In themselves. They led through a darkened passage
To a brightness he'd only dreamed of but could see
As an intricate beginning and end of light
Which turned and burgeoned forward and floated away
As if entranced by the other side of music.

In his joy he joined that dance. He knew without seeing
That she was dancing too on the rock-strewn stairway,
And only after he'd turned for the third time
Did it dawn on him she was no longer there.

Night at the Zoo

In the smallest hours of the night they climb the walls
    Of the zoo, over the barbed wire
        And through the dark shrubs and roses, scuttling
Along deserted paths, keeping to shadows,
    Past closed concession stands, bringing with them
        No cameras, no children for amusement,
Looking for no fast food. The watchmen
    And keepers call them *nightcrawlers*
        And find them in the beams of flashlights,
Their eyes turned bright, crouching
    And blinking. Some are staggering
        Drunk, needing a place to sleep, and some
Are fraternal boys who have pledged themselves
    Once too often to ride on elephants
        Or camels, and some are thieves
Wanting to wrap rare birds and reptiles
    In muslin bags and carry them away,
        And some declare ferociously
Their love for everything alive and forgive
    Their trespass as the right of endangered wildlife
        Asserting the freedom to lie down
Like lambs among the bears or lions
    Or the great apes, to take their places
        Finally in some natural habitat
Between the arms and legs, the claws and teeth
    Of their lost companions of the night
        Of the fifth day of God,
And some of these the keepers only discover
    At the dawn of the sixth day
        Like the lonely man who climbed
Down to the dry moat between the guardrail
    And the icy pool with its concrete terraces
        In the polar bears' enclosure, leaving a message

Above the warning sign—*We must get closer*
    To the animals. He was found sprawled
        Between the forepaws of one sleepy brother
Who had grown tired of playing with his body
    After slapping and shaking him to a peaceable,
        Agreeable, and respectful silence.

Elegy for Some of My Poems

Some were stillborn. For them, a moment of silence.

Others died so soon after birth
(Siamese triplets, microcephalic odds
Without ends, the offspring and outfall
Of incompatible species) their freakishness
Is half-concealed now by their innocence.

Some died early, victims of malnutrition,
Overexposure, and gross neglect. A motherless few
Were smothered by strangers.

And two consisted wholly of parts from the graves
Of the recently dead. When brought dimly to life
By heat lightning and static electricity,
They merely jerked and shuddered a moment,
Then fell off the gurney.

Of those who lived to hear their voices break,
Some throttled themselves and died in fits of outrage,
And some drowned in a rapture of the depths
At the shallow end of the pool of Narcissus.

Several in mid-career escaped hanging
By the skin of their wits and died later
Of a lingering green-sickness. Some breathed their last
Blindfolded, up against the wall, half-shot at dawn.

Of the rest, the less said, the better,
Since they had almost nothing to say themselves.

My once dearly beloved, you are gathered together here
In the sight of your maker, under the covers
Of a common grave, in rows, now left to your own devices,
With the sure uncertain hope you may go back
To the loam of the mother of language
To be rearranged for the seeds of a better father.

Plainsong against the Raising of the Dead

No doubt they were all missed
To start with, but at last,
These men and women have been
Unanimously dismissed.
They have all been excused
For being absent. Their services
Are no longer required.
Half have been half-forgotten
And the other half forgiven.
Their chairs and vanities,
Desk drawers and parking places,
And the wrong sides of their beds
Have been filled by others. They have
The right to remain silent.

Why would we want them here?
Some would come back half-blind
Befuddled aphasic ghosts
Foot-dragging their ways home
Red-handed, groaning all night,
Inarticulate to the bone,
Their already softened features
Bedraggled into blurs.

And some would be heartsick
Over the crossed-out years
With the bitter aftertaste
Of old lives in their mouths,
And some, their swollen faces
Swelling more out of rage
At our necromantic gall,
Might want to break or wring
Our necks instead of our hearts.

And suppose their bodies and griefs
Could somehow be redressed:
They would be none the wiser.
What beautiful ugly lies
Or truths could they tell us
That we hadn't already told
Ourselves about Rebirth
And Death after Death after Death?
There would be so much love
Lost between us now,
We couldn't imagine it.

And the few who could genuinely
Be said to know what to do
With a second turn at the wheel
Of fortune, another burning
Kiss good-bye by the fire,
Odds are, would spend their sweet
Choice interval killing time
Or bottles or enemies
Or audiences of one
Or houseflies or themselves.

They have no need of us.
They've agreed at length with the earth.
They've gone the way of all breath.
Better to keep our distance,
To make our ritual
Observances to the moon
Or the good stars or bad weather,
To tend to the flowering
Of the dust over their names
Remembering what they were
In the morning of their years
And hoping the cold rain
Falls gently where they are.

At the Summit

One more half-step, another half
    And a half, and as far as you can see
        Or tell, blinking around you, nothing
Is higher than you or your head
    But a few clouds. You're not exactly standing,
        But you're on the top of a mountain,
On bare, wind-etched rock
    Nearly as smooth as ice. You're so short
        Of breath, you crouch over your lungs
As if to give them shelter. You'd cheer
    If you had almost enough breath
        To blow out a candle or could light
A candle if you had one. You'd try to sing
    If you could think of a song or dance
        If you could move. Or hug somebody
If you had another body or yourself
    At least to keep warm. You'd say something
        Memorable if you could
Remember anything, and you'd laugh
    If only the corners of your mouth would turn
        Up and come open and your belly
Give the old, old heave-ho
    To something besides ice water as old
        And as cold as when it ran the other way
Down your throat. You want to believe
    In joy. It would be too terrible
        If you could only think of it
In the meantime. The rocks at your feet
    Seem as commonplace as your boots.
        They're not thinking of themselves
As above it all. The heart of the earth
    Has thrust them onto this summit
        Without discussing the matter in advance.
And before long, they'll be washed or blown or shaken
    Away, brushed off and down the rubble-strewn slopes
        To be cracked and shattered,

To take their turns as bits of a mob scene,
       And though you could always leave something behind
              For the next climber to stumble across,
Some weatherproof memento like your ice-axe
       Or your bones or an empty bottle, it seems
              A slovenly gesture. All the way
From the foot of the mountain to this pinnacle,
       You've had less and less room to maneuver,
              To choose or change, but here at last your mind
Has been changed for you. Like a man at the North Pole
       Who can only go south, you can only go
              Back down, slipping away.

Planting a Red Maple

Sale: All bare-root trees 50% off!
—sign at a garden store

They all look dead, lined up like bad examples,
An inch thick and eight feet tall: delinquents
In a tough house of correction, with ID tags
Marked down, all pruned and crimped, their desiccated
Stubs of roots in plastic. But their labels
Are full of full-color promises of success,
Adults in full bloom, full leaf, the fulfilled dreams
Of amateur landscapers.
                              I lift one maple
And shake it. It's so close to being a stick,
How can it know what it is? The roots seem
Barely supple and springy enough, if bent
From their set ways, to keep from breaking.
Are these hard buds alive? Does it still know
How to begin again? Is it stuck with being
Only what it remembers, repeating one story:
The dream of waking, the struggle upward,
The buds, the leaves, the blossoms, the first fruits,
Horse manure, being uprooted and cut short
By some routine disaster in a nursery?
I take it home and dig it a place to stand
And spread its roots in a stiff truncated calyx
And baptize, brace, refill, and do a slow
Flatfooted round shuffle to seal our compact.

Will it suffer my neglect and contrary help,
The unintentional oversupply of sun
And rain, the inexcusably cold snow, the smut
And fungus, the close attentions of leaf-rollers?
Will it send down and out those curious fibers
Nothing can follow between and among stones
And sand grains and loam, the alleys and dead ends
And melted worlds and star clusters of mud?

Will it lift up and open its leaves like wings
Turning to fire, to spread over a garden
Its broad branches graced with multiple lives
Whole mornings and afternoons and evenings
And nights in a dance of hours? Will its share of keys
Come spiraling down to all the other kingdoms?

For a Row of Laurel Shrubs

They don't want to be your hedge,
        Your barrier, your living wall, the no-go
                Go-between between your property
And the prying of dogs and strangers. They don't

        Want to settle any of your old squabbles
                Inside or out of bounds. Their new growth
In three-foot shoots goes thrusting straight
        Up in the air each April or goes off

                Half-cocked sideways to reconnoiter
Wilder dimensions: the very idea
        Of squareness, of staying level seems
                Alien to them, and they aren't in the least

Discouraged by being suddenly lopped off
        Year after year by clippers or the stuttering
                Electric teeth of trimmers hedging their bets
To keep them all in line, all roughly

        In order. They don't even
                Want to be good-neighborly bushes
(Though under the outer stems and leaves
        The thick, thick-headed, soot-blackened

                Elderly branches have been dodging
And weaving through so many disastrous springs,
        So many whacked-out, contra-
                Dictory changes of direction, they've locked

Themselves together for good). Yet each
        Original planting, left to itself, would be
                No fence, no partition, no crook-jointed
Entanglement, but a tree by now outspread

With all of itself turned upward at every
       Inconvenient angle you can imagine,
And look, on the ground, the fallen leaves,
       Brown, leathery, as thick as tongues, remain

       Almost what they were, tougher than ever,
Slow to molder, to give in, dead slow to feed
       The earth with themselves, there at the feet
       Of their fathers in the evergreen shade

Of their replacements. Remember, admirers
       Long ago would sometimes weave fresh clippings
       Into crowns and place them squarely on the heads
Of their most peculiar poets.

Acknowledgments

Poems in the "New Poems" section of this book have appeared in the following periodicals in the years shown:

Poetry: "A Summer Storm in Navarre, Ohio," "In the House of the Dragon," "Planting a Red Maple," "A Letter Home," "For a Row of Laurel Shrubs," "Plainsong against the Raising of the Dead," and "The Silence of the Stars," 1997; "Recital," "The Return of Orpheus," "At the Summit," "Going Back to the Sea," and "In a Garden," 1998
Shenandoah: "In the Shadow" and "Looking for Shiva in the Public Market," 1997
Seattle Review: "Elegy for Some of My Poems," 1997
Ontario Review: "The Young Goats" and "Night in the Zoo," 1998
Virginia Quarterly Review: "Alexandra and the Spiders," 1998
Triquarterly: "Recitation," 1998

Illinois Poetry Series
Laurence Lieberman, Editor

History Is Your Own Heartbeat
Michael S. Harper (1971)

The Foreclosure
Richard Emil Braun (1972)

The Scrawny Sonnets and Other
Narratives
Robert Bagg (1973)

The Creation Frame
Phyllis Thompson (1973)

To All Appearances: Poems New
and Selected
Josephine Miles (1974)

The Black Hawk Songs
Michael Borich (1975)

Nightmare Begins Responsibility
Michael S. Harper (1975)

The Wichita Poems
Michael Van Walleghen (1975)

Images of Kin: New and Selected
Poems
Michael S. Harper (1977)

Poems of the Two Worlds
Frederick Morgan (1977)

Cumberland Station
Dave Smith (1977)

Tracking
Virginia R. Terris (1977)

Riversongs
Michael Anania (1978)

On Earth as It Is
Dan Masterson (1978)

Coming to Terms
Josephine Miles (1979)

Death Mother and Other Poems
Frederick Morgan (1979)

Goshawk, Antelope
Dave Smith (1979)

Local Men
James Whitehead (1979)

Searching the Drowned Man
Sydney Lea (1980)

With Akhmatova at the Black Gates
Stephen Berg (1981)

Dream Flights
Dave Smith (1981)

More Trouble with the Obvious
Michael Van Walleghen (1981)

The American Book of the Dead
Jim Barnes (1982)

The Floating Candles
Sydney Lea (1982)

Northbook
Frederick Morgan (1982)

Collected Poems, 1930–83
Josephine Miles (1983; reissue, 1999)

The River Painter
Emily Grosholz (1984)

Healing Song for the Inner Ear
Michael S. Harper (1984)

The Passion of the Right-Angled
Man
T. R. Hummer (1984)

Dear John, Dear Coltrane
Michael S. Harper (1985)

Poems from the Sangamon
John Knoepfle (1985)

In It
Stephen Berg (1986)

The Ghosts of Who We Were
Phyllis Thompson (1986)

Moon in a Mason Jar
Robert Wrigley (1986)

Lower-Class Heresy
T. R. Hummer (1987)

Poems: New and Selected
Frederick Morgan (1987)

Furnace Harbor: A Rhapsody of the
North Country
Philip D. Church (1988)

Bad Girl, with Hawk
Nance Van Winckel (1988)

Blue Tango
Michael Van Walleghen (1989)

Eden
Dennis Schmitz (1989)

Waiting for Poppa at the Smithtown
Diner
Peter Serchuk (1990)

Great Blue
Brendan Galvin (1990)

What My Father Believed
Robert Wrigley (1991)

Something Grazes Our Hair
S. J. Marks (1991)

Walking the Blind Dog
G. E. Murray (1992)

The Sawdust War
Jim Barnes (1992)

The God of Indeterminacy
Sandra McPherson (1993)

Off-Season at the Edge of the World
Debora Greger (1994)

Counting the Black Angels
Len Roberts (1994)

Oblivion
Stephen Berg (1995)

To Us, All Flowers Are Roses
Lorna Goodison (1995)

Honorable Amendments
Michael S. Harper (1995)

Points of Departure
Miller Williams (1995)

Dance Script with Electric Ballerina
Alice Fulton (reissue, 1996)

To the Bone: New and Selected
Poems
Sydney Lea (1996)

Floating on Solitude
Dave Smith (3–vol. reissue, 1996)

Bruised Paradise
Kevin Stein (1996)

Walt Whitman Bathing
David Wagoner (1996)

Rough Cut
Thomas Swiss (1997)

Paris
Jim Barnes (1997)

The Ways We Touch
Miller Williams (1997)

The Rooster Mask
Henry Hart (1998)

The Trouble-Making Finch
Len Roberts (1998)

Grazing
Ira Sadoff (1998)

Turn Thanks
Lorna Goodison (1999)

Traveling Light: Collected and
New Poems
David Wagoner (1999)

Some Jazz a While:
Collected Poems
Miller Williams (1999)

National Poetry Series

Eroding Witness
Nathaniel Mackey (1985)
Selected by Michael S. Harper

Palladium
Alice Fulton (1986)
Selected by Mark Strand

Cities in Motion
Sylvia Moss (1987)
Selected by Derek Walcott

The Hand of God and a Few
Bright Flowers
William Olsen (1988)
Selected by David Wagoner

The Great Bird of Love
Paul Zimmer (1989)
Selected by William Stafford

Stubborn
Roland Flint (1990)
Selected by Dave Smith

The Surface
Laura Mullen (1991)
Selected by C. K. Williams

The Dig
Lynn Emanuel (1992)
Selected by Gerald Stern

My Alexandria
Mark Doty (1993)
Selected by Philip Levine

The High Road to Taos
Martin Edmunds (1994)
Selected by Donald Hall

Theater of Animals
Samn Stockwell (1995)
Selected by Louise Glück

The Broken World
Marcus Cafagña (1996)
Selected by Yusef Komunyakaa

Nine Skies
A. V. Christie (1997)
Selected by Sandra McPherson

Lost Wax
Heather Ramsdell (1998)
Selected by James Tate

So Often the Pitcher Goes to Water
until It Breaks
Rigoberto González (1999)
Selected by Ai

Other Poetry Volumes

Local Men and *Domains*
James Whitehead (1987)

Her Soul beneath the Bone:
Women's Poetry on Breast Cancer
Edited by Leatrice Lifshitz (1988)

Days from a Dream Almanac
Dennis Tedlock (1990)

Working Classics: Poems on
Industrial Life
*Edited by Peter Oresick and Nicholas
Coles* (1990)

Hummers, Knucklers, and Slow
Curves: Contemporary Baseball
Poems
Edited by Don Johnson (1991)

The Double Reckoning of
Christopher Columbus
Barbara Helfgott Hyett (1992)

Selected Poems
Jean Garrigue (1992)

New and Selected Poems, 1962–92
Laurence Lieberman (1993)

The Dig and *Hotel Fiesta*
Lynn Emanuel (1994)

For a Living: The Poetry of Work
*Edited by Nicholas Coles and Peter
Oresick* (1995)

The Tracks We Leave: Poems on
Endangered Wildlife of North
America
Barbara Helfgott Hyett (1996)

Peasants Wake for Fellini's *Casanova*
and Other Poems
*Andrea Zanzotto; edited and translated
by John P. Welle and Ruth Feldman;
drawings by Federico Fellini and
Augusto Murer* (1997)

Moon in a Mason Jar and *What My
Father Believed*
Robert Wrigley (1997)

The Wild Card: Selected Poems,
Early and Late
*Karl Shapiro; edited by Stanley Kunitz
and David Ignatow* (1998)

Typeset in 9.5/13 Palatino
with Palatino display
Designed by Paula Newcomb
Composed at the University of Illinois Press
Manufactured by Maple-Vail Book Manufacturing Group